Copyright

interpreting the law for
libraries, archives and
information services

Every purchase of a Facet book helps to fund CILIP's advocacy, awareness and accreditation programmes for information professionals.

Copyright

interpreting the law for
libraries, archives and
information services

REVISED SIXTH EDITION

Graham P. Cornish

facet
publishing

© Graham P. Cornish 1990, 1997, 1999, 2001, 2004, 2009, 2015, 2019

Published by Facet Publishing
7 Ridgmount Street, London WC1E 7AE
www.facetpublishing.co.uk

Facet Publishing is wholly owned by CILIP: the Library and Information
Association.

British Library Cataloguing in Publication Data
A catalogue record for this book is available from the British Library.

ISBN 978-1-78330-423-3 (paperback)
ISBN 978-1-78330-424-0 (hardback)
ISBN 978-1-78330-425-7 (e-book)

First published 1990
Second edition 1997
Third edition 1999
Revised third edition 2001
Fourth edition 2004
Fifth edition 2009
Sixth edition 2015
This revised sixth edition 2019

Text printed on FSC accredited material.

Typeset from author's files in 10/14pt American Garamond and Function
by Flagholme Publishing Services.

Printed and made in Great Britain by CPI Group (UK) Ltd, Croydon
CR0 4YY.

Contents

Author's note

This book tries to set out the basics of United Kingdom (UK) copyright law, concentrating on those areas which may affect libraries, archives, museums and galleries in their daily work. For the sake of brevity this group of organisations will be referred to collectively as 'libraries', although whenever this term is met it should be interpreted as including all four types of organisation. Some areas have not been dealt with at length if they do not relate directly to libraries, and the whole area of design and patents is left to others far more competent to deal with in those areas where they impinge on the work of libraries. Neither is it intended as a scholarly textbook but rather as a working tool for the practitioner who is faced with actual situations which need to be resolved in an informed and sensible way. Therefore references to case law or even specific clauses of the legislation are not included. The book can be used as a desktop reference work for anyone planning library and information services or kept at the enquiry desk to help decide what can, or cannot, be done for a user. The author's hope is that it will be as helpful to junior counter staff as to senior managers. It is also aimed at staff in all types of library and information service, whether public, academic, government or private. Attention is given to the different legal situations in which various libraries function. As would be expected, the book focuses on UK law, which it aims to interpret, and the answers found here should never be assumed to apply in other countries. Nevertheless, many of the questions raised are equally valid in any part of the world and should help professionals in other countries to address the issues facing their own libraries.

As libraries and information providers increasingly move towards exploiting their collections or providing new information services, there is a need to look at what rights libraries and others enjoy when they create a work, as well as when they wish to use something. Digitisation programmes in particular raise many challenging questions and some of these will be dealt with in this book.

The book comprises questions and answers to simplify searching for particular problems and their possible solutions. Because of this there is a small amount of repetition between sections. This is deliberate in order to avoid unnecessary 'see also' comments, which tend to confuse or bewilder the user. Obviously not every possible question can be answered but every effort has been made to anticipate those which arise most often. The feedback from many users of previous editions of this book has been most useful in expanding and amplifying some of the paragraphs in this edition. The law is not there to deal in specific terms with any and every possible situation but to provide the framework within which decisions can be made in specific circumstances. There are always 'grey' areas of interpretation or circumstance when the law is unclear. Where this is the case, the book tries to offer guidance rather than provide a definite answer, as this is not always possible.

Much of the legislation is untried in the courts and interpretation may necessarily be a little 'fuzzy'. Other areas are much more specific and can make interpretation easier but implementation more difficult!

It should be remembered that what the law does not allow can often be achieved with the copyright owner's consent through an appropriate licence. Therefore, where the book says that the law prevents something, librarians should first check to see what kind of licence, if any, is available for copying beyond the stated limits. For this reason a chapter on licences has been included in the sure and certain knowledge that it will soon become out of date in such a fast-moving area. In a book of this kind it is not possible to say exactly what existing licences allow, as they differ between different types of institution and change with time, but indications have been given as general guidance.

Leaving the European Union (Brexit)

This revised edition is being prepared as negotiations continue about how and when the UK will leave the EU. The impact of this on copyright laws is therefore uncertain but it seems likely that no major changes to copyright law as it affects libraries will happen until the end of 2020. However, the government has prepared a Statutory Instrument which will come into force on the day the UK leaves the EU. This makes some changes to geographical interpretations of the current law, such as replacing 'European Economic Area' or 'EU member states' with 'United Kingdom'. In the event of the UK leaving the EU at an early date, users of this book are advised to check this instrument for any changes. There may also be some changes relating to the use and digitisation of orphan works.

About the author

The author has worked in the field of copyright since 1983 and advised the British Library on copyright matters for 18 years. He has run workshops and seminars in many different sectors of the information industry. He now works as an independent adviser and trainer in all aspects of copyright under the label ©opyright Circle. The wealth of information and opinion gathered from his contacts has been used to compile this book but it must be remembered that it is written by a librarian trying to understand the law, not a lawyer trying to understand libraries!

Disclaimer

While the advice and information contained in this book are believed to be true and accurate at the date of going to press, neither the author nor CILIP can accept any legal responsibility or liability for any errors or omissions that may be made. Nothing in this book constitutes formal legal advice.

Graham P. Cornish
©opyright Circle
Harrogate

Acknowledgements

Nobody knows everything about copyright. Consequently, anyone who writes a book on the subject must be indebted to others working in the field. This is certainly true of this author and I would like to thank particularly Tim Padfield, formerly of The National Archives (TNA), for his wisdom on every aspect of archives; Charles Oppenheim, formerly of Loughborough University, for his challenging alternative interpretations of the law; various members of the Libraries and Archives Copyright Alliance; and, above all, the many people who have taken part in the numerous copyright workshops throughout the country at which I have taught and whose questions have so enriched this edition.

My thanks also go to my friend and long-standing colleague, Stella Pilling, for proofreading my text.

List of abbreviations

CCC	Copyright Clearance Center
CCLI	Christian Copyright Licensing International
CDPA	Copyright Designs and Patents Act 1988
CLA	Copyright Licensing Agency
DACS	Design and Artists Copyright Society
EEA	European Economic Area
ERA	Educational Recording Agency
FOI	freedom of information
HMSO	Her Majesty's Stationery Office
IPO	Intellectual Property Office
IPR	intellectual property right
ISBN	International Standard Book Number
ISSN	International Standard Serial Number
JISC	Joint Information Services Committee (now known as Jisc)
MPLC	Motion Picture Licensing Corporation
NLA	Newspaper Licensing Agency
OCR	optical character recognition
OS	Ordnance Survey
OU	Open University
PLR	Public Lending Right
PRS	Performing Right Society (now PRS for Music)
PPL	Phonographic Performance Ltd
SI	statutory instrument
TNA	The National Archives
UCC	Universal Copyright Convention
USGPO	United States Government Printing Office
VAT	value added tax
VLE	virtual learning environment

Introduction

The 1988 Copyright Designs and Patents Act (CDPA) and the many subsequent statutory instruments (SIs) which interpret and modify it differ substantially from the Copyright Act, 1956. However, some aspects of this old Act still apply to some materials, as do some clauses of the 1911 Act, so they should not be ignored completely. Many definitions have changed and new rights have been introduced. Licensing as a concept is now also a major feature of information delivery but it was in its infancy in 1988.

Users are asked to note that some of the terms used in the Act are not ones that the author would choose to use. Particularly the term 'disabled person' is one that is controversial, but this is the term used in the law so it has been used throughout the book.

The introduction of new legislation often has the effect of heightening awareness of the subject, making people keener to know their rights and privileges and generally creating an atmosphere of extreme caution in case anyone puts a foot wrong and ends up in court. While this is a good thing, nobody should become too paranoid. Although there has been a recent tendency for copyright infringement cases to be heard in criminal courts, this is usually where important commercial considerations apply, such as republishing or reproduction in bulk for commercial purposes. Criminal proceedings may also be taken for circumventing or tampering with electronic rights management systems. Most infringements of copyright by individuals are dealt with through the civil courts, if events reach that stage, so that the rights owner must take legal proceedings if it is thought an infringement has taken place. As there are no cases at present involving libraries in the UK, it would be reasonable to assume that a similar route would be taken, given that libraries are not, or should not be, involved in mass reproduction for commercial gain!

The Act and its supplementary legislation also set the stage for a completely new approach to the use of copyright material. We may know what the law says (even if we do not always know what it means!) so there is now the necessity to develop services outside the exceptions which the Copyright Act makes by talking to the licensing agencies and other rights owners' organisations to negotiate use of material in return for royalties. Those working in the information industries should not lose sight of this as a real way forward when the law inhibits the introduction of new services without the owners' consent. Licences granted by copyright owners should override the limitations set by the law but in most cases cannot override the privileges given to libraries by Parliament.

The sixth edition of this book appeared in 2015 as a result of seismic changes to copyright law in the UK which came into force in 2014. This revised edition brings that up-to-date and includes some minor changes which have taken place as a result of clearer interpretation. The one major change that has taken place is a negative one: the original 2014 legislation allowed copying of an item for personal use by the owner of the item: for example, converting a video to a DVD or a vinyl recording to a CD. This was struck down by the courts for various reasons and the government decided not to try to re-introduce it.

These changes are the reason for a revised edition. There is an extensive index, a list of useful addresses and websites, and suggestions for further reading.

Section 1
Definition and law

1.1   What is copyright?

Copyright is part of a batch of rights, usually called intellectual property rights (IPRs), given to the creators of various types of works. Which right is found in a work depends on its nature but the major strands to IPR are patents, trade and service marks, design right, registered design and copyright. These can overlap to some degree and more than one right may be found in a work. This book concentrates on copyright.

Because it is a property right, copyright is governed by the usual rules of property. The owner can sell it, lend or rent it, leave it in a will or just give it away; similarly others can buy or hire it through licences or other agreements. The idea behind copyright is rooted in certain fundamental ideas about creativity and possession. Basically, it springs from the idea that anything we create is an extension of 'self' and should be protected from general use by anyone else. Coupled with this is the idea that the person creating something has exclusive rights over the thing created, partly for economic reasons but also because of this extension of 'self' idea. Copyright is therefore important to ensure the continued growth of writing, performing and creating generally. If there were no copyright protection there would be little stimulus for people to create anything, as other people would be able to take the work and use it in any way they wanted. This mirrors the usual rules of possessing property. Copyright law aims to protect this growth but, at the same time, tries to ensure that some access to copyright works is allowed as well. Without this access creators would be starved of ideas and information to create more copyright material.

1.2   Is copyright a monopoly?

Not entirely. If two people create the same thing independently of each other and without actually copying what the other person wrote or made, then both can claim copyright in what they create, even if they are identical.

Example: Two people stand in exactly the same place and take a photograph. The photos are virtually identical but each photographer owns the copyright in their photo because they did not copy someone else's work.

1.3   Why is copyright important for libraries?

Libraries are in a unique position as custodians of copyright material. They have the duty to care for, and allow access to, other people's copyright works. This places special responsibilities on all those working in libraries and the information world generally. We practise our profession by using this property so we should take all possible steps to protect it, while at the same time ensuring that the rights and privileges of our users and our profession are also safeguarded.

1.4   Why is copyright so often ignored by users?

Because it is such an intangible thing, there is often a temptation to ignore it. Those who take this approach forget that they, too, own copyright in their own creations and would feel quite angry if this were abused by others. Some of the restrictions placed on use by the law may seem petty or trivial but they are designed to allow some use of copyright material without unduly harming the interests of the creator (author). With the rapid growth of social networks, individuals are becoming more aware of the value of their creations such as photos and poems.

1.5   Is copyright valuable in terms of financial value?

In the UK copyright is primarily a property right intended to protect the rights of those who create works of various kinds. The protection is intended to prevent exploitation of their works by others. It follows that copyright cannot exist by itself but only within the work which has been created. For this reason we say that copyright 'subsists' rather than exists. Because it is a property it has value. That value will be determined by market forces and how the owner rates it as a valuable resource.

1.6   So, is copyright just about cash?

No, authors also need to protect their personal rights, regardless of money. These rights are outlined in Section 3.

1.7   What is the latest legislation?

The basic piece of legislation is the Copyright, Designs and Patents Act 1988 (CDPA), which came into force on 1 August 1989. There is also the Exploitation and Regulatory Reform Act 2013, which gives the secretary of state various powers to change some aspects of copyright. The CDPA has to be read in conjunction with a number of subsequent SIs and the supporting regulations. There are a number of these but the laws and statutory instruments (SIs) which affect libraries most are:

Copyright, Designs and Patents Act 1988

SI 92/3233 Copyright (Computer Programs) Regulations 1992

SI 95/3297 Copyright Rights in Performances: the Duration of Copyright and Rights in Performances Regulations 1995

SI 96/2967 Copyright and Related Rights Regulations 1996

SI 97/3032 Copyright and Rights in Databases Regulations 1997

SI 2003/2498 Copyright and Related Rights Regulations 2003

SI 2005/223 The Copyright (Educational Establishments) Order 2005

SI 2006/18 The Performances (Moral Rights etc.) Regulations 2006

SI 2006/346 Artist's Resale Right Regulations 2006

SI 2013/777 The Legal Deposit Libraries (Non Print Works) Regulations 2013

SI 2013/1782 The Copyright and Rights in Performances Regulations 2013

SI 2014/898 Copyright (Regulation of Relevant Licensing Bodies) Regulations 2014

SI 2014/1372 Copyright and Rights in Performances (Research, Education, Libraries and Archives) Regulations 2014

SI 2014/1384 Copyright and Rights in Performances (Disability) Regulations 2014

SI 2014/1385 Copyright (Public Administration) Regulations 2014

SI 2014/1457 The Public Lending Right Scheme 1982 (Commencement of Variations) Order 2014

SI 2014/2356 Copyright and Rights in Performances (Quotation and Parody) Regulations 2014

SI 2014/2588 Copyright and Rights in Performance (Extended Collective Licensing) Regulations 2014

SI 2014/2863 Copyright and Rights in Performances (Licensing of Orphan Works) Regulations 2014

SI 2016/1219 Copyright and Performances (Application to Other Countries) Order 2016

Digital Economy Act 2017

SI 2018/995 Copyright and Related rights (Marrakesh Treaty, etc.)
(Amendment) Regulations 2018

Note that the texts of all this legislation can be found on the website www.legislation.gov.uk, so extracts are not reproduced in this book. Go to this website for the text of Acts of Parliament and SIs.

Note that the government consulted on changing rules for unpublished materials but decided against taking any action in 2015.

It is important to note that a number of terms used in the legislation are not defined. It is also worth noting that some SIs that interpret what the Act says simply give more detail than the Act itself can do. SIs that implement European directives are far more complicated and may remove parts of the Act, modify other parts and certainly introduce new sections and clauses. So never just look at the original Act itself. The latest batch of SIs (2014) radically changes parts of the Act and introduces completely new material.

1.8 So, if I have all this legislation in front of me, can I work out what the law means?

No! In addition to the many SIs, you need to bear in mind that the language in the Act is full of undefined terms, and case law frequently changes the way we understand the meaning of the Act.

1.9 How can I keep up with the changes to the law?

There are some suggestions in the list of useful sources of information at the end of this book to help with this problem.

1.10 Which terms are undefined?

These terms are undefined: 'original', 'substantial(ly)', 'reasonable' (and 'reasonably'), 'librarian' or 'archivist', 'fair dealing', 'periodical', 'commercial research', 'public' (and 'publicly').

1.11 Are there definitions of some terms?

Yes. There are sections of the Act devoted entirely to defining words used in the Act itself. But some definitions are contained in the section of the Act to which they relate. Important terms include 'article', 'copy' and 'copying', 'curator', 'museum', 'conducted for profit' and 'disabled person'.

1.12   Does the law apply to the whole of the UK?

Yes, but remember that the Isle of Man and the Channel Islands are not part of the UK. Jersey and Guernsey are now included as part of UK ratification of the Berne Convention and have enacted various regulations on copyright. The Isle of Man passed its own copyright legislation in 1991 so the copyright part of this Act (Part 1) does not apply there. Also the Isle of Man is now covered by the database legislation. In addition, some aspects of remedies for owners relating to infringement and some of the criminal aspects of copyright are handled differently in Scotland because of the different way that Scots law works in these areas. It is to be hoped users of this book never have to investigate these!

1.13   Any other catches?

Yes, some phrases and words mean different things in different parts of the law. For example 'making available to the public' has several different meanings, as does 'publish'.

Section 2
What is covered by copyright?

2.1 **What things are covered by copyright?**

Virtually anything that is written, expressed in graphic form or recorded in any way, or anything that can be made by a human being, but not usually things made by a mechanical process, is capable of being protected by copyright. The law divides these items into various classes and all aspects of them are dealt with separately in the following pages.

2.2 **Does absolutely anything in these groups qualify for copyright?**

No. There are three tests to qualify for copyright and any work must pass all three. They are that the work must be original, recorded and created by a qualifying person.

2.3 **What does 'original' mean?**

The law does not say, but the idea is that, to be protected, the author must have contributed quite a lot of their own ideas or skills to the making of the work. Works that are merely trivial will not qualify, as they do not demonstrate any originality. Anything that is merely a copy of something that already exists cannot be protected by copyright as a new work.

2.4 **What constitutes 'trivial'?**

This is not defined but a primitive doodle or a simple 'x' would not qualify, although what is 'simple' and what is not is open to debate!

2.5 **When does a work based on another work become original?**

When sufficient time, effort, technical skills and knowledge have been used to make it reasonably clear the work is a new one and not merely a slavish copy.

Example: If you write your own poem about Jack and Jill, it is protected. If you simply reproduce the well-known nursery rhyme with one or two minor changes, the reproduction is not original and not protected – but if you photocopy or scan a printed version of the poem the typographical arrangement may be protected (see Section 4.88 and following).

2.6   What about digitisation and the images which it produces?

This is an area where the law is unclear. Generally speaking, it is held that if the work is digitised using a scanner and there is no human intervention (like a photocopy and producing a PDF file that cannot be manipulated) then there is unlikely to be any new copyright work created. So a mere scanned copy may not be protected by copyright but an image that has had a lot of work carried out on it to enhance its appearance, correct the text or change the colouring – using optical character recognition (OCR) type technology – probably will be protected.

2.7   So, if the library digitises some old parts of its collection, can it benefit at all from copyright?

If the images are enhanced, probably. But even if they are not, the actual collection of images may qualify for database right (see Section 9) if they are organised in a systematic and methodical way.

2.8   What does 'recorded' mean?

Fixed in some way, such as writing, or using any form of notation or code; stored in a computer system; recorded on a disc (vinyl, CD, CD-ROM); or recorded on a film (including video and DVD). A live performance, which is not recorded or videoed, for example, would not attract copyright because it ceases to exist as soon as it is delivered. There is nothing to show what it contained or what it was like, so it cannot be copied, nor can the person who delivered it show what was in it.

2.9   Can copyright subsist even if the original work has disappeared or been destroyed?

Yes. If, for example, a painting was photographed and then destroyed, there would still be copyright in the original painting, even though it did not exist, through the existence of the photograph. There would also be copyright in the photograph.

2.10   Which authors qualify for copyright protection?

The person claiming to be the author must be a UK citizen or a citizen of a country where UK works are protected in the same way as in the UK (see Sections

12.1 and following). A complete list of these countries is given in the SIs listed in Section 1. Also anyone carrying out work for the Crown, Parliament, the United Nations or the Organization of American States has that work protected as if it were published in the UK, even if the author is a national of a country not otherwise covered by these arrangements. See also Section 4.101 and following. If the author is not a national of one of these countries, but publishes the work in a country that is covered by these arrangements, then the work is protected as if published in the UK.

If there is no author the work must have been published in a country that protects works in the same way as the UK does.

2.11 Is there copyright in facts or ideas?

No. A fact is a fact and cannot be protected in itself. However, the way in which information about facts is presented is protected. Similarly, ideas are not protected, only the expression of them.

Examples: Times of trains are facts and nobody can prevent you from publishing information that trains leave at certain times for particular places. What is protected is the layout of the timetable and the actual typography. So you might make this information available by including it in a brochure about a tourist attraction but it would be an infringement to reproduce the timetable and reprint this in the brochure.

Similarly the idea for a computer game is not protected but the way it is expressed (icons, graphics, instructions, underlying software) is. Therefore competing games can be produced but not using the same elements.

2.12 Is the title of a book or journal article protected by copyright?

Rarely. Such titles are statements of fact – they tell you what the book or article is called – and cannot therefore be protected unless they are so complex that they become a literary work in their own right or are registered as a trademark. In this case the problem would arise only if the 'make-up' of the new work looked so like the first work that one could be mistaken for the other. How many journals called *Impact* or *Update* do you know?

2.13 What about works which are illegal, such as pornography?

Just because a work is pornographic, libellous or irreligious does not mean it is not protected by copyright. On the other hand, courts have sometimes refused to uphold copyright in such works where a claim for infringement has occurred, because circulation of it was not in the public interest. The problem is, as always in such matters, that what is pornographic today may be entirely acceptable tomorrow. Thus there will be copyright in such works but it may be difficult to enforce.

2.14   Are things like trademarks and logos protected by copyright?

Yes. A logo is an artistic work and a trademark may well be an artistic work and/or a literary work as well. It is possible for a trademark to go out of copyright but still be a trademark, as trademarks can last indefinitely. Therefore it could be legal to copy an old trademark provided it was not used to market a similar product. For example it might be possible to illustrate a book on advertising with pictures of out-of-copyright trademarks, but not use the same trademark for products sold in a museum shop showing retail life 100 years ago.

2.15   Are any works excepted from the usual copyright protection?

Yes. The King James Version of the Bible (also referred to as the Authorised Version), the *Book of Common Prayer* of the Church of England and Sir James Barrie's *Peter Pan* all enjoy special protection outside normal copyright limitations. The Authorised Version of the Bible and the *Book of Common Prayer* are printed under patents issued by the Crown and are therefore in perpetual copyright. This does not extend to modern versions, which must be treated as published works that are anonymous, whatever one's personal theological view! The Authorised Version of the Bible and *Book of Common Prayer* cannot be copied, as they are outside copyright law. Permission is usually given for small quotations in publications, and photocopying of various portions for research or private study or reading in church or chapel is usually allowed. In the case of *Peter Pan*, ironically, the Copyright Act brought in perpetual copyright in this play for the benefit of the Hospital for Sick Children, Great Ormond Street, London, provided it remains as a hospital. The Hospital owned the copyright, which expired on 31 December 1987, and obtained a considerable revenue from it. Parliament decided to continue this privilege and any commercial publication or performance of the work attracts a royalty for the Hospital. This is a form of compulsory licensing for a work now out of copyright. As the Act did not come into force until 1 August 1989, any act of copying, commercial publication or performance carried out between 31 December 1987 and 31 July 1989 was not an infringement. The play cannot be publicly performed without royalty payment to the Hospital for Sick Children. As this law applies only to the UK it causes considerable confusion for the film industry, which is free to exploit it outside the UK but not import products derived from it into the UK without a licence from the Hospital.

In addition, some items, such as patents, qualify technically for copyright, but an international agreement between patent offices has waived all protection of patents for non-commercial copying.

Section 3
Rights and limitations

This section looks at what rights authors and owners of copyright enjoy under the law.

3.1   What is the difference between authorship and ownership?

Authors and owners may, or may not, be the same person. They enjoy different rights, so the distinction is important. As authors are defined differently for different types of work, they will be dealt with separately under each heading. However, despite some variations, their moral rights are similar in most circumstances so they will be covered in this section. This section then sets out who the owner is and what the owner is entitled to do exclusively in law. The rights enjoyed by authors are called 'moral rights' and are generally very weak in UK law. On the other hand, owners enjoy a whole range of rights which are economic in nature. The limitations to these rights are then dealt with in Section 4.

Moral rights
3.2   What are moral rights?

Moral rights are designed to protect the idea that anything created contains an element of 'self' in it. Therefore the author ought to be able to protect certain aspects of a work. Although the law is complex in this area and most library services may not think they have major concerns with moral rights, the growth of electronic information sources, Open Archives, Creative Commons and similar systems makes an understanding of moral rights important for all information services.

3.3   What are these rights?

Essentially they give the author the right to protect their work from being abused or their reputation from being sullied.

3.4 **What specific rights do authors have?**

Basically, authors have a right to prevent their work being distorted by additions, deletions or changes to its meaning. They also have the right not to have works they did not create attributed to them and prevent anyone else claiming to be the author of their work. They also have the right to prevent their work being used in a way that would bring their reputation into disrepute.

3.5 **What about making sure their name is included in a work?**

Rather surprisingly, this is not an automatic right of the author. It applies in certain contexts only and will be dealt with under each type of copyright material in the following sections. In summary, it applies only to authors of monographs, producers and directors of films and artists whose work is to be exhibited in public.

3.6 **Do all authors enjoy moral rights?**

No. Anyone who creates anything as part of their employment forfeits virtually all moral rights to their employer. See Sections 3.14 and following.

3.7 **Do moral rights last for the same length of time as other rights?**

Yes, but with one important exception. The right not to have works falsely attributed to oneself lasts for only 20 years from the end of the year in which the person dies.

Ownership of copyright

3.8 **Who owns copyright?**

Although authorship and ownership are quite different roles in copyright law, they may be fulfilled by the same person; where this is the case, it is important to distinguish these two roles. Ownership of copyright is a complex question. Copyright is a property and can be disposed of in the same way as other property, so ownership is not always easy to identify. The author may have assigned the copyright to someone else. It may have been sold to a publisher, given to someone else, left to someone in a will or automatically transferred to an employer, the Crown or Parliament. In 1996 the law changed, extending copyright protection in many cases from 50 to 70 years after death. This gave rise to 'extended' copyright (where 20 years has been added on to existing copyright) and 'revived' copyright (where a work was out of copyright because the author had been dead for more than 50 years, but because they had been dead for less than 70 years copyright came back into force).

3.9 **Is the copyright in a work one single piece of property or can it be broken up?**

Copyright is a complicated bundle of rights (see Section 3.32 and following) and these can be assigned or licensed to different people. For example, the author of a book may license publication in hardback to one publisher, paperback to another, distribution in different parts of the world to different publishers again, making of an audio version to yet another company and film rights to someone else entirely. They can also be licensed for a limited period so that one person may have one bundle of rights for 10 years, then acquire a licence for them for a further 30 years and so on. This is particularly important for works made into films or plays, musicals, operas and ballets. The matrix of copyright ownership is very complex.

3.10 **Are there any rules for transferring copyright?**

Yes, an assignment of copyright, by which the owner passes over some or all of their rights *exclusively* for a specified period, must be in writing. Unless this assignment is in writing there is no transfer of copyright. This is very important for contracts.

3.11 **What is the difference between an assignment and a licence?**

An assignment transfers the management of copyright to someone else, usually for a given period and for specified purposes. During that time the original owner cannot exercise any of the rights transferred under the assignment. Assignment is normally exclusive. Licences are quite different. They do not transfer any rights but allow other people to share in the rights of the owner (for example, to copy a work), but the original owner retains all their rights and the licensee does not gain any rights, only permissions. This is a feature of copyright management that is different from managing other types of property.

3.12 **Someone must start the ownership process. Who owns copyright first?**

Copyright is usually owned first of all by the author.

3.13 **Why usually?**

Because there are different rules depending on employment or commissioning.

3.14 **How does employment come into ownership?**

If authors create a work as part of their job, then their employer is usually the owner. However, there can be a contract between employer and employee which states the opposite (the copyright remains with the employee). See the notes on commissioned works in the following paragraphs. There are special arrangements for Crown and Parliamentary copyright (see Sections 3.27 and following). Also the author is differently defined for different classes of works such as films and sound recordings. Most of the legislation is actually about the rights enjoyed by the owner of copyright rather than the author. For this reason most authors' economic rights are referred to as 'owners' rights'.

3.15 Supposing the work was commissioned?

If the work was commissioned after 1 August 1989, the copyright is owned by the author. Before that date, copyright in commissioned paintings, engravings and photographs is usually the property of the person who commissioned the work, provided they paid for the work to be done. Copyright in other types of commissioned works remains with the person creating the work. As with works created as part of employment, a contract in writing can transfer copyright to the commissioner.

3.16 Does 'commissioned' mean the author had to be paid?

Yes, but this is important now only for artistic works mentioned in the last paragraph.

3.17 What about documents such as minutes of meetings for clubs, societies and churches when the secretary is not employed but is a volunteer?

The most probable situation is that, although the secretary may have put their name on the minutes, the right to exploit those minutes belongs to the club, society or church. They would enjoy the equity in them even though the secretary could rightly claim to be the author.

3.18 Supposing a library owns an original work such as a manuscript. Does the library own the copyright?

No. It is important to distinguish between the object and the copyright which subsists in it. The library may own the manuscript but the copyright is still owned by the author or the person to whom it has been assigned, so the library has no right to reproduce the manuscript, except as allowed by the exceptions in the Copyright Act. However, the library may enjoy other rights over the manuscript under publication right (see Sections 4.91 and following).

3.19   Who owns the copyright in a work bequeathed to a library or archive?

There is a special additional exception for unpublished works. When an author leaves unpublished manuscripts or other materials of which they are the author to a library, archive or museum as a bequest, and their will does not specify any other arrangements, the presumption is that the copyright is also transferred to the library, archive or museum. They may specify differently in the will; if they do, this will affect the way the unpublished material can be used. If the work is deposited by the author during their lifetime, or deposited by the family, but copyright is not assigned to the library or archive, then copyright remains with the author or their heirs and successors.

3.20   Can the library acquire the copyright?

Yes. When it buys the manuscript, painting and so on it is possible to buy the copyright as well. Again, this must be under contract in writing. Glasgow City Council owns the copyright in the painting by Salvador Dali called *Christ of St John of the Cross* because it bought it with the painting and any reproduction of that painting has to be sanctioned by Glasgow City Council.

3.21   Who owns the copyright in a letter?

The author – the person who wrote the letter, not the archive that holds the letter or the recipient of the letter.

3.22   Why does the person who received the letter not own it?

Because copyright belongs to the person who creates the work. The letter itself does belong to the person who received it. She or he was given it by the writer. But the copyright still belongs to the writer, not the recipient, of the letter.

3.23   What about a letter sent to the editor of a newspaper or journal?

Technically the copyright still belongs to the writer of the letter although, by sending the letter to the editor in the first place, there is an assumption that the writer wished it to be published and therefore the editor has an *implied* licence to publish. This does not give the editor or the publisher any other rights over the use of the letter.

3.24   Who owns the copyright in a periodical issue?

Each author of an article in a periodical issue owns the copyright in that article, but the publisher owns the copyright in the issue as a whole, including the typographical arrangement (see Sections 4.88 and following)

Example: Someone writes an article for a periodical. Unless they sign an agreement to the contrary, they retain the copyright in the article and have the right to have it published elsewhere. But they do not have the right simply to photocopy the article as first published and have it republished in that form. This would infringe the typographical copyright of the publisher. (Nor do they have the right to make copies of the whole periodical issue.) For the same reason the author cannot simply make multiple photocopies of the article for friends and colleagues. Contracts between authors and publishers can vary enormously and some allow much more liberal use or reuse of material than others.

3.25   Who owns 'extended copyright'?

Essentially the person who owned the copyright immediately before the extended copyright came into force (see Sections 3.8 and following).

3.26   Who owns 'revived' copyright?

The person who owned the copyright immediately before it expired. If that person is dead, or the body owning the copyright has ceased to exist, then the copyright is owned by the personal representatives of the author (see Sections 3.8 and following).

3.27   Who owns Crown copyright?

Crown copyright is explained in more detail at Sections 4.85 and following. Technically, the Crown. However, Crown copyright is administered by Her Majesty's Stationery Office (HMSO), which, although now privatised, still has a residual responsibility to administer copyright owned by the Crown.

3.28   Who owns the copyright in a Parliamentary bill or Act of Parliament?

The copyright in a bill belongs to whichever House introduced the bill first. When the bill becomes an Act it becomes Crown copyright. The copyright in other materials belongs to whichever House first commissioned the work to be done. Similar rules apply to Scotland and Northern Ireland but they are slightly different for Wales.

3.29   Supposing a work is out of print. Does the publisher still own the copyright?

This will depend on the contract between the author and the publisher; generally speaking, copyright in a work reverts to the author if the work goes out of print and the publisher has no plans to reprint or republish the work. However, the publisher will retain the copyright in the typography of the work (see Sections 4.88 and following).

3.30   Who owns the copyright in children's work in schools?

Despite the general myth that it is owned by the school, the child who creates anything in school owns the rights in it and it cannot be used for any purpose without the child's (or guardian's) permission.

3.31   What about published children's poems or pictures in magazines or school brochures?

Permission must be sought from the child or guardian.

3.32   What rights does the law give the copyright owner?

Copyright law gives the owner exclusive rights to do certain things to or with the copyright material. Nobody else is entitled to do these things. There are seven basic rights:

- to copy the work
- to issue copies to the public
- to perform, show or play the work in public
- to adapt or translate the work
- to rent out or lend the work
- to communicate the work to the public by electronic means
- to make recordings of performances available.

Each of these rights will be examined under the appropriate type of work. Those who own rights in databases or performances have a different set of rights.

3.33   Are these absolute rights or do other people have some rights to use the material as well?

They are not absolute, because they are limited by quantity, time, purpose and certain exemptions given to user groups. Each of these limitations will be examined under the appropriate type of work. But it is important to note that the limitations set for use of copyright material are, in many cases, no longer exceptions to the rights of owners but rights enjoyed by users.

Quantity

3.34   Is the whole and every little bit of a work protected?

No. Copyright is limited by excluding from protection less than a substantial part of a work. So if less than a substantial part is used or copied there is no infringement except in certain areas.

3.35   What constitutes a substantial part?

Substantial is one of those undefined words. What is clear is that it is not just a question of quantity but quality as well.

Example: Someone copies the recommendations and conclusions (three paragraphs) from a 70-page technical report. This is almost certainly a substantial part. Similarly four bars of a symphony could constitute a substantial part because they encapsulate the theme music of the whole work. In one case 30 seconds from a one-hour broadcast was considered a substantial part.

3.36   Are there any guidelines?

Not really. Each case must be a matter of professional judgement.

Time

3.37   Does copyright last for ever?

No, but the rules relating to just how long it does last are very complex. They will be dealt with for each type of copyright material in the following sections.

Purpose

Where users of copyright material are given certain rights to use the work without permission from the copyright owner, these are called 'exceptions'.

3.38   Can these exceptions be blocked by copyright owners?

Those relating to libraries and also education and quotations cannot be overridden by the copyright owner. Note that any clause in a contract that tries to limit the exercise of these exceptions is considered null and void. For example, the statement in some books that 'No part of this work may be copied' has no status in law and cannot be enforced.

3.39 For what purposes can copyright material be used without asking permission?

The law gives several main reasons:

- for fair dealing
- for public administration
- to make temporary copies
- for educational use
- to meet the needs of disabled people.

These will be dealt with for each type of copyright material in the following sections.

User groups

3.40 Are any exceptions made for particular user groups or needs?

The law gives special exceptions and privileges to three user groups:

- those working in or undertaking education
- libraries, archives, museums, galleries and their users
- disabled persons.

Orphan works

3.41 What if the copyright owner cannot be identified or found?

This gives rise to what are currently referred to as 'orphan works', where it is not possible to identify who either the author or the publisher actually was, or these can be identified but neither they nor their successors can be traced. In these circumstances the best advice is to make all reasonable inquiries to find the copyright owner's whereabouts but, if all fails, then it is necessary to contact the Intellectual Property Office (IPO), which operates a licensing scheme for the use of orphan works. The government has produced guidelines on how to go about tracing copyright owners and what will constitute 'reasonable inquiry'. See www.gov.uk/government/publications/orphan-works-diligent-search-guidance-for-applicants for details.

3.42   **So can nothing be done with orphan works except through a licence?**

Yes, because the rules about copying for education, fair dealing and preservation still apply whether the work is an orphan or not. Also there are special rules about manuscripts held in libraries which can be copied for research or private study or even with a view to publication. See Section 4.112 for details.

Section 4

Literary, dramatic and musical works

4.1 **Why are these three grouped together?**

Because they are all treated in a similar way under the Copyright Act, although there are some differences for some specific areas. In addition, a printed and published text also has a copyright in the typographical arrangement of the work concerned, regardless of the copyright status of the content. Any literary work that also qualifies as a database is subject to special rules. See Section 9 for details.

Definitions

Literary works

4.2 **What is a literary work?**

The term 'literary work' includes anything made up of words or characters that are written in any form, such as books, journals, technical reports and manuscripts, and covers any works that are spoken or sung provided they are recorded in some way. It also includes compilations (where these do not qualify as databases – see Section 9) as well as computer programs and text stored electronically. The handwritten notes of an author are protected just as much as the final printed book.

4.3 **Does 'literary' mean it has to be good-quality literature?**

No. Copyright law says almost nothing about the quality or content of the work, although case law shows that trivial works are not eligible for protection. Literary means anything that is written, spoken or sung which has been recorded, whether in writing or some other notation or code. This is why a computer program is considered a literary work in legal terms. It also includes items such as knitting patterns.

4.4   **What about books or articles written in scripts like Japanese, Chinese or Arabic, which many people in cultures using the Latin alphabet cannot read?**

This makes no difference. They meet the criteria of being written in a notation or code. Just because some people cannot read them it does not mean others cannot! People whose language is recorded in scripts other than the Latin alphabet will have the same view.

4.5   **What about databases? Are these covered by copyright?**

They may sometimes be covered by copyright but they are definitely covered by database right as a separate type of work. See Section 9 for details.

4.6   **Are bibliographic records covered by copyright?**

This is a difficult question and has never been clarified in law. The question is: Is a bibliographic record 'original'? Originality requires some intellectual input from the author. Most bibliographic records consist of a series of facts presented in a pre-determined order according to pre-determined cataloguing codes of practice. In theory, everyone using these codes should produce exactly the same record. The fact that they do not is more to do with human fallibility than the rules themselves! It has been held that merely to follow exact instructions does not give the person actually doing the work any copyright in the work they create. For example, an architectural draughtsman following exact design instructions is not considered to have made a new copyright work. It is difficult to decide whether a catalogue record has any copyright as such, although the typography in any physically published catalogue would be protected (see Sections 4.88 and following).

4.7   **Are bibliographies not protected by copyright?**

Almost any bibliography will qualify as a database rather than a literary work and must be treated accordingly. The one exception is the scholarly bibliography, which may be annotated and is prepared by one identifiable person. See Section 9 for detailed information.

4.8   **Is a library catalogue protected?**

A library catalogue is almost certainly a database and will be protected as such. See Section 9.

Dramatic works

4.9   What is the difference between a literary and a dramatic work?

A dramatic work is the non-spoken part of a presentation, which gives instructions as to how the play is to be executed. The words of a dramatic work are protected as a literary work. The term 'dramatic work' also covers choreography, dance and mime.

Example: A show like *West Side Story* has separate copyrights in the words (literary work), the choreography and the directions (dramatic work) and the music (musical work). But see Section 4.118 for works where the music and the words are meant to go together.

Musical works

4.10   Does musical work mean anything with music included?

No. Musical work means only the notes on the stave and excludes the words (which are a literary work) and any actions which go with the music, because they are dramatic works.

Example: *West Side Story* (as mentioned above in 'Dramatic works') will have three separate copyrights: in the words; in the actions and movements of the dancers; and in the musical notes. Although this may sound complicated it is important because the people who composed the three elements will each own a separate copyright which may expire at different times. So the music might go out of copyright but not the words, or vice versa. But see Section 4.118 for works where the music and words are meant to go together.

4.11   Does musical work include a recording of the music?

No. That is separately covered as a sound recording (see Section 6).

4.12   What about a play performed and recorded on video?

The play is protected as a literary work and the video made of the performance is protected as a film, quite separately. The performers will also have separate rights in their performances. See Section 7.

Authorship

Definition of author

It is important to define who the author of a work is, as this usually determines how long copyright lasts. Term of copyright is most often linked to the death of the author. It is also important to note that the author is defined differently for different types of material.

4.13   **What is the definition of the author?**

For literary, dramatic and musical works it is the person who created the work.

4.14   **Does the author have to be a human person or can it be a company or organisation?**

The author must be a human being ('natural person' in legal terms). If no human author is identified the work is considered anonymous.

4.15   **What about a song where the words and music are composed to go together?**

When a work is made up of words and music which were created in order to be used together then these are called works of co-authorship.

4.16   **Supposing there are two or more authors?**

They all count as the author of the copyright.

4.17   **Supposing it is not possible to find out who the author is?**

A work is considered anonymous if the identity of the author cannot be traced by making reasonable inquiries.

4.18   **What does 'reasonable inquiry' mean?**

This is not defined but the government has issued guidelines as to what constitutes a diligent search for the author or copyright owner. See Section 3.41.

4.19   **What happens if the author's identity is established later on?**

Once the author's identity is established, then the work is no longer anonymous and the usual procedures apply.

4.20   **Supposing the author has used a pseudonym?**

Unless you can find out whose pseudonym it is, then the work is counted as anonymous. As with anonymous works, this would require reasonable inquiry – checking of literary reference works and major library catalogues. See Section 4.128 for an example.

4.21   **What happens if a work definitely has more than one author, but not all their names are known?**

Once the name of even one author is known, the work is no longer anonymous.

4.22   **Supposing the author is given as an organisation?**

If no natural (human) person is named as the author the work is treated as anonymous.

4.23   **If a work was generated by a computer, who counts as the author then?**

The person who made the necessary arrangements for creating the work (but see Section 9).

4.24   **What about compilations such as directories, timetables, bibliographies and encyclopedias?**

If the work has a personal author then that person is the author. So a bibliography compiled by a named person is protected just as if it were a book. However, something like the *British National Bibliography* has no personal author so is protected only as a database. Most works like this qualify as databases (see Section 9), for which separate rules apply.

4.25   **What about works which have lots of articles by different people, such as an encyclopedia, which has articles signed by separate people?**

Then each article is protected as a separate work, and the work as a whole may also be a database.

4.26   **Supposing some articles are signed and some not?**

They are all treated separately as individual works, so copyright in some will be treated as the work of an author and some will be anonymous.

Authors' rights

4.27   **Do authors of literary, dramatic and musical works all enjoy moral rights (as described in Section 3)?**

It depends on the type of material. Authors of monographs (books) and directors of films have the right to have their name included when the work is published.

This right has to be asserted in writing. Authors of other works in this group do not have this right.

However, authors of works in this group do have the right to prevent derogatory treatment of their work (see Sections 3.4 and following).

Ownership

4.28   Who is the owner of copyright in a literary, dramatic or musical work?

The basic rules are set out in Section 3 but there is a special additional exception for unpublished works. When an author leaves their unpublished manuscripts or other materials to a library as a bequest and their will does not specify any other arrangements, then the presumption is that the copyright is also transferred to the library. They may specify differently in the will and, if they do, this will affect the way the unpublished material can be used.

Owners' rights

4.29   What rights do owners of copyright in literary, dramatic and musical works have?

Essentially copyright is an exclusive right against which certain exceptions are set to make a balance between owner and user. This section begins by looking at the rights which owners of copyright enjoy and then examining how they are limited by exceptions.

Copying

4.30   Does the owner alone have the right to make copies?

Yes, subject to the limitations mentioned later on.

4.31   Does copying just mean photocopying?

Certainly not. It means copying in any material form. This includes any method of copying, including resetting the type to make a new edition for publication, copying by hand or taking a photograph. Photocopying is clearly copying something and there are special provisions to allow some types of copying for some purposes. It also means electronic copying, which includes storing a work in any form and copying the text onto a computer disk, converting it to electronically readable text using scanning equipment of various kinds, storing it on CD-ROM or transmitting it by fax. This also includes making copies of computer programs for any purpose.

4.32 What else constitutes copying?

Any action which uses the actual text that someone else has written, even if it is then changed. When someone takes a piece of another author's work and makes out it is their own (plagiarism) then that is copying as well. The courts distinguish between actual copying and using someone else's ideas but not their actual text. So Dan Brown's famous work *The Da Vinci Code* was held to be based on the ideas in another book but did not actually copy the text, so it did not infringe copyright.

4.33 Using a computer, especially the internet, also involves copying. Is this not allowed either?

This involves temporary copies, which are necessary for the technical procedures involved. The law specifically says that such copies are not infringing so we can surf the internet without any anxiety! See Section 11.37 for more details.

4.34 Fax involves copying. Is the use of fax really an infringement?

As the law allows the making of temporary copies which have no independent significance, it would seem likely that merely sending a fax which produced nothing more than a paper copy at the other end would not be an infringement. However, if the process resulted in a stored electronic copy being generated and available for subsequent use then this would probably be an infringement

4.35 Documents received by fax sometimes fade and disappear. Can the document be further copied as soon as it is received to make a durable copy?

Not legally. Unlike the temporary copy made by a fax transmission, this is a permanent copy so further copies should not be made. An exception might be a copy faxed for interlibrary loan purposes so that the faxed copy might be further copied for preservation purposes.

4.36 What about microforms?

Making a microform is copying and is not permitted without the owner's consent. See Section 5.4 for more detailed information.

4.37   Can copies be made for committee meetings?

No. Copying for committees is multiple copying and is not permitted unless the amount copied is less than substantial. However, in many organisations committee copying would be covered by an appropriate licence.

4.38   Can a slide or image for a PowerPoint presentation be made of a page of a book for teaching in a class or giving a lecture?

Yes. The copying must be fair to the copyright owner; the copy must be made by the person giving or receiving instruction; the copying must be for a non-commercial purpose; and the source must be acknowledged where possible.

4.39   Some books and journals carry a warning that no part of the work can be reproduced, stored, etc. Does this take away the allowances given under the Copyright Act?

The law states that any form of contract that seeks to prevent the use of exceptions for the benefit of the user is null and void. This would therefore cancel out any such statement. More recent books by properly informed publishers preface this prohibitive statement with the phrase 'Except as otherwise permitted by the relevant copyright law . . .'.

Issuing copies to the public

4.40   Is issuing copies to the public the same as publishing?

This is essentially what we would think of as traditional publishing but note that the issue to the public does not have to be for money. Even if you distribute copies of someone's copyright work for free it is still an infringement of their right to do this or authorise others to do it.

4.41   If issuing copies to the public is an infringement, how can libraries offer a lending service?

The law makes it clear that the right to issue copies to the public only applies to works that have not previously been made publicly available in the European Economic Area (EEA). So, once a work is published in the EEA it can be lent within the specific provisions for the lending and rental of copyright material (see 'Lending and rental' under each type of material).

4.42 Does this idea of issuing copies to the public have any bearing on acquisition of materials by a library?

Essentially, no. If the work has been made legally available within the EEA then it can be legally acquired by a library, even if imported from another country. Any responsibility for infringing importation would rest with the bookseller involved, not the library. Libraries occasionally import single copies but these are not for commercial purposes, so infringement is unlikely.

Performing rights

4.43 What are performing rights?

Every author has the right to decide if a work shall be performed in public, whether it is a recitation of a poem, extracts from a book, or delivery of a speech. The author also has the right to decide whether the performance can be recorded. The performer has this last right too.

4.44 What about exhibiting a work. Does that count as performance?

Rather bizarrely the answer is yes. So it would be an infringement to display a manuscript, which was still in copyright, to the general public in an exhibition, but not other types of material.

4.45 Is this really important for libraries and archives?

Libraries are increasingly involved in cultural activities and some have library theatres, so it is important to be aware of the owners' rights, especially when library materials may be used to put on performances. This includes plays, concerts and arts festivals generally. Increasingly libraries and archives arrange poetry readings and sessions in which stories are read to children as well.

4.46 Can only the copyright owner authorise performance?

Yes, although it may be done through a licensing agency (see Section 10) or an author's agent.

4.47 Does performance mean just plays or presentations?

No. Performance includes delivery of speeches, lectures or sermons and also includes presentation by visual or audible means.

Example: If the library possesses some poems by a local author, they may not be copied. But it is also an infringement to recite them in public or make a video of someone reciting them in public. For example, family videos of weddings may infringe the copyright in the vicar's sermon if reading from a prepared text. However, if the vicar is speaking extempore, there is no copyright in the sermon until it has been recorded (on the video). The vicar then owns the copyright in the sermon and the person who shot the video owns the copyright in the video!

4.48   Does this mean that poems cannot be used for public recitation?

Not quite. One person may read a reasonable extract from a copyright work in public provided that the reading is accompanied by sufficient acknowledgement.

4.49   What do the terms 'reasonable extract' and 'sufficient acknowledgement' mean?

They are not defined. Reasonable extract is a matter of judgement. Sufficient acknowledgement would certainly mean saying who wrote the work, and when and where it was published, if published at all.

4.50   What about story-telling for children in libraries?

Technically this is an infringement by performance (see Sections 4.45 and following).

4.51   Sometimes teachers want to perform plays or hold concerts using copyright library materials. Is this allowed?

Yes, provided that only students, teachers and other persons directly connected with the educational establishment are present. This does not include mums and dads!

Communicating the work to the public by electronic means
4.52   What exactly does this mean in practical terms?

This right is defined as 'communication to the public by electronic transmission', which includes:

* broadcasting the work
* making the work available by electronic transmission so that members of the public may access it from a place and at a time individually chosen by them.

This clearly includes putting material on a website. See Section 8 for broadcasts.

4.53   Does this have any implications for libraries and archives?

As far as literary, dramatic or musical works go, the main fact to bear in mind is that broadcasting a work is an infringement of the owner's rights. So if a local radio station wished to use some of the library's holdings for broadcasting purposes, such as poems, musical compositions or extracts from local history material, this would not be allowed without permission. This would not apply if the use were solely for news reporting.

4.54   Does this have any effect on the use of websites?

Yes. The definition of this right makes it clear that putting anything on a website without the copyright owner's permission is an infringement.

Adaptation and translation

4.55   Does adaptation apply just to plays, novels or similar materials?

No. It includes translation, adaptation, conversion of dramatic works to non-dramatic works, and turning a story into a cartoon or similar work. Translating a work is considered an adaptation and translations should not be made without due consideration for the purpose for which they are made and the use to which they will be put.

4.56   What can be done for a researcher in the laboratory of a company who needs a technical article translated?

As the use would be for a commercial purpose, the translation can be made only with the consent of the copyright owner.

4.57   What about a student who wants to translate a play in a foreign language?

If the student makes their own translation there is unlikely to be a problem but they must not publish it or make it available on the internet.

4.58   What is the position regarding religious texts?

Any translation of a religious text may be protected by copyright. If it is the work of a specific translator then the usual rules about how long copyright lasts will apply. If the translation is the work of a panel or group then it will be regarded as anonymous and the rules for anonymous works will apply. The original text from which the translation was made will probably be out of copyright anyway, unless it is very recent, so then anyone can make their own translation and distribute it.

4.59 Is it an infringement to re-write a non-dramatic work as a dramatic one and vice-versa?

Yes. It is also an infringement to reproduce a story in another form, such as pictures.

    Example: Someone decides to re-work Alan Ayckbourn's *The Norman Conquests* as a novel. This is an infringement. Equally it would be an infringement to produce a dramatic version of one of Catherine Cookson's novels.

4.60 Does this restriction include turning a story into pictures, for example for a children's library?

Yes. The law specifies that it is not allowed to turn the story into a version wholly or mainly told in the form of pictures suitable for reproduction in a book, newspaper or magazine. Although this is obviously aimed at the cartoon market, it has implications for children's libraries and school libraries as well.

4.61 How does the rule on adaptation affect arrangements of musical works?

Any arrangement of a transcription of a musical work counts as an adaptation. In one case the notation of a 17th-century musical work was changed so that it could be understood by modern musicians although the actual music produced remained the same. This was considered an adaptation (and also a new work).

4.62 Does 'translation' extend to computer 'languages'?

Yes. The law specifically states that changing a program from one computer language to another is an infringement unless this is done incidentally during the running of the program. But see Section 11.

4.63 Supposing an adaptation or translation has been made legally. Does that also attract copyright?

Yes, and the person who made the adaptation has rights in the adaptation just as the author has in the original work. The owner of the original work may also have an interest in the copyright of the adaptation made.

Lending and rental

4.64   Who is allowed to lend or rent copyright works to others?

Lending and rental are exclusive rights of the copyright owner but the rules governing them are complicated and many acts of lending are not considered as 'lending' for legal reasons.

4.65   What is actually meant by 'lending'?

The meaning of lending is defined in the legislation as follows:

- a work is made available for use on the presumption that it will, or may be, returned
- the lending does not lead to any economic or commercial advantage to the lender
- the work is lent by an establishment that is accessible to the public or by a qualifying library (see Sections 4.195 and following) that is not conducted for profit, but by a public library only if the work is covered by the Public Lending Right Act or was acquired before 1 December 1996.

Lending does not include:

- making available for public performance
- performing in public
- broadcasting
- making available for exhibition purposes
- on-the-spot reference use
- making available between establishments accessible to the public.

4.66   Does this mean that a library which lends material cannot charge?

No. The necessary operating costs of the lending establishment may be recovered. Where lending takes place in these conditions it is not defined as 'lending'!

4.67   What about organisations which are not accessible to the public?

Lending undertaken by them is not within this legislation and is not therefore considered 'lending' in legal terms, even if it is in general terms.

4.68   What does 'on the spot' mean?

This is not defined but it would seem clear that use of a work within a library or similar collection where the work is not taken out of the room would clearly be on the spot. Whether taking a work from one room in a building to another or from one building to another within a single site still constitutes on the spot is not clear. It seems unlikely that 'the spot' would be stretched to use on a different site.

4.69   Which libraries can lend material?

As educational establishments can lend any material it would seem likely that the library of any such establishment could lend material to another library.

4.70   What about other libraries?

Any library which is a qualifying library (see Sections 4.200 and following) and which is not conducted for profit can lend material, so presumably it can be lent to other libraries.

4.71   What about public libraries?

As public libraries can lend only material within the Public Lending Right (PLR) Scheme they can lend only these items to other libraries.

4.72   What can public libraries lend?

Since 1 December 1996 public libraries can lend:

- any printed materials obtained before 1 December 1996
- only materials acquired after 1 December 1996 which are covered by the PLR Scheme or which would have been eligible for coverage by the scheme because of their form but are precluded because of country of origin, date of the author's death, or other similar reasons.

4.73   What works would qualify under this last, rather confusing, definition?

To try to clarify this, a new edition of a book by an author who died over 70 years ago is not eligible for PLR but would have been if the author had died recently. To avoid the situation where the public library could not lend this book because it is outside the PLR scope, it can be treated for lending as if it is eligible even though it is not!

4.74 **What about books without authors, such as directories or bibliographies?**

These can be for reference only, if acquired after 1 December 1996.

4.75 **What about periodicals, maps or photographs?**

If acquired after 1 December 1996 they must be for reference only.

4.76 **What about lending works through interlibrary loan?**

Care may be needed here. Lending between establishments which are accessible to the public is not counted as lending. But there are specific clauses dealing with libraries, which will probably override this general exception, as the normal practice is that where specific regulations exist they take precedence over general rules.

4.77 **Can any library take part in interlibrary loan arrangements?**

It depends whether the library is being asked for copies or is asking for copies and whether the library wishes to lend or borrow.

4.78 **Which libraries can lend to other libraries?**

There is no legislation which deals directly with lending between libraries. 'Lending' is defined as not including 'making available between establishments which are accessible to the public', but the term 'accessible to the public' is not defined, and there are separate clauses for lending from libraries which are not just establishments accessible to the public. However, some possible situations in which interlibrary loan can take place can be deduced.

4.79 **What do these special arrangements permit?**

These allow any qualifying library (see Sections 4.200 and following for a definition of this term) that is not conducted for profit to lend copyright works. As lending is defined as not being for economic or commercial gain, the charging for this interlending should not cost more than the operating costs to carry out the lending. So a commercial or industrial library cannot lend but they can borrow such items from other non-profit prescribed libraries.

4.80 **If a work has been borrowed by a library can it then be lent to an end-user?**

It would seem that this will depend on whether that library can lend this type of material to end-users from its own collection. If lending from its own collection would not be allowed it is unlikely that it could lend material from another collection which it could not lend from its own collection. For example, public libraries cannot lend issues of periodicals so it would seem unlikely that a public library could borrow a back issue from another library (say, an educational library) and lend that to an end-user, when it cannot lend the same type of material from its own collection.

4.81   What about libraries in commerce and industry?

If the library is not accessible to the public then what the library does is not considered lending for copyright purposes. However, if the library is accessible to the public, any library in this category cannot lend any material but it might be able to borrow from other libraries. However, it would not be able to lend the material borrowed as such libraries are not allowed to lend.

4.82   What about libraries in charities or other organisations?

If they are accessible to the public then they are bound by the rules as set out above. If they are not accessible to the public, then presumably they can lend, as what they do is not considered lending from a copyright point of view.

4.83   What constitutes rental?

Rental is making something available for a limited time on the expectation that it will be returned and for which a charge above the necessary operating costs is recovered.

4.84   Can libraries have rental schemes?

Libraries can have rental schemes only with the agreement of the copyright owner.

Crown and Parliamentary copyright
4.85   What is Crown copyright?

When a work is created by an employee of the Crown it becomes subject to Crown copyright, which is technically owned by the Crown (Her Majesty), and different rules apply to this type of material.

4.86   Who counts as a Crown employee?

Since the distancing of much civil service work from central government and recent moves to devolution this is no longer clear. Major government departments and ministries are Crown employees but the status of many bodies (for example the British Library and national museums) is that they are not Crown employees, even if they are owned and funded by the government. A full list of what organisations are and are not Crown employees can be found on TNA website (see 'Useful addresses and contacts' for details).

4.87   What is Parliamentary copyright?

Parliamentary copyright exists in any work commissioned by either or both Houses of Parliament.

Typographical arrangements of published editions

4.88   What is typographical copyright?

Every published work has two copyrights: one in the actual content of the text and the other in the printed layout of the page. The latter is typographical copyright.

4.89   What is the point of these two copyrights?

If a publisher publishes or re-publishes a work that is out of copyright, such as Shakespeare's plays, they still have some protection for their efforts in setting up the typography and producing the book, even though the actual content can be freely published by someone else.

4.90   Who counts as the author of the typographical arrangement of a work?

The publisher.

Publication right

4.91   What is publication right?

Publication right is similar to, but distinct from, copyright. It gives exclusive rights in the work to the first publisher. It was introduced on 1 December 1996.

4.92   Does publication right exist in all works?

No, but it can exist in any literary, dramatic, musical or artistic work, or a film.

4.93   When does it exist?

Publication right exists when anyone in the EEA first publishes a work that:

- is out of copyright
- is published by someone who is an EEA citizen
- has not been previously published in the UK or any EEA state.

For a list of countries that are members of the EEA see Section 4.102.

4.94   Does 'published' mean published commercially?

No. In the context of publication right (and the definition is different in different contexts) it means communication to the public (an undefined term) and in particular:

- issuing copies to the public
- making the work available by means of an electronic retrieval system
- renting out or lending copies to the public
- performing, showing or exhibiting in public
- broadcasting.

4.95   When does an unpublished work go out of copyright?

See Sections 4.110 and following for details, but note that unpublished literary, dramatic and musical works of which the author had died before 1 January 1969 are protected for 50 years from the date when the new law came into force (1989) and therefore do not come out of copyright until 31 December 2039, the first date on which publication right for these classes of works can come into force. Unpublished works of which the author died after 31 December 1968 enjoy the usual 70 years protection unless the author is a national of a non-EEA country, in which case copyright lasts for as long as that country provides protection. Note that the government carried out a consultation on simplifying these rules in 2015 but decided not to make any changes.

4.96   Does this mean that where publication right comes into force, libraries and archives lose control of unpublished material in their collections?

Fortunately, no. The publication can take place only with the consent of the owner of the physical material in which the work is recorded. So a library or archive could refuse to allow a work to be published or permit it only under strict conditions (including royalties!).

4.97   Are there any works that are subject to publication right now?

No. Not until 31 December 2039.

Making available right

4.98   Does making available right apply to literary, dramatic and musical works?

This right, which is the equivalent to communicating the work to the public by electronic means, applies only to the performances of them.

Duration of copyright in literary, dramatic and musical works

4.99   Does copyright last for the same period for all literary, dramatic and musical works?

No. There are different periods of copyright as described below.

Published works

4.100   What constitutes 'published'?

'Published' means issuing copies to the public. This in turn means putting into circulation copies not previously put into circulation. Note that the emphasis is on copies. Making a single copy does not of itself constitute publication. The definition also includes making the work available through an electronic retrieval system.

4.101   How long does copyright last for published literary, dramatic and musical works?

This depends on the country of origin of the work. If the work was published in an EEA country (see Section 4.102 for a list of countries the EEA covers), or the author is an EEA national, then the copyright in published literary, dramatic or musical works lasts for 70 years from the end of the calendar year in which the author dies. Copyright always expires on 31 December, never in the middle of a year.

Example: Author died on 5 January 1942. Copyright expires on 31 December 2012. Author died on 29 December 1942. Copyright still expires on 31 December 2012.

4.102   Which countries are members of the EEA?

As at September 2019, the European Economic Area comprised Austria, Belgium, Bulgaria, Croatia, Cyprus, Czechia [Czech Republic], Denmark, Estonia, Finland, France, Germany, Greece, Hungary, Iceland, Ireland, Italy, Latvia, Liechtenstein, Lithuania, Luxembourg, Malta, Netherlands, Norway, Poland, Portugal, Romania, Slovakia, Slovenia, Spain, Sweden and the UK.

4.103   What about works published outside the EEA?

These are protected for the same length of time as they would be in their own country if none of the authors is an EEA national. If a work is published in a country which gives only 50 years protection then that is all it will get within the EEA.

4.104   Supposing a work was published simultaneously in several countries both within and outside the EEA?

In this case, it is considered an EEA publication. Note that 'simultaneous' means within 30 days of first publication. So a work could be published in, say, Australia one day but, provided it was also published in an EEA country within 30 days of that first publication, it would still qualify for EEA protection.

4.105   Supposing the work is anonymous or has no personal author?

Anonymous works first published within the EEA, which includes works which have no personal author such as annual reports of organisations, or anything with no identifiable personal author, remain in copyright for 70 years from the end of the year in which they are created. If they are published during that period then the 70-year period starts all over again. Otherwise the work is protected for the length of time it would have been protected in the country of origin (usually 50 years).

4.106   Does it make a difference if the author died before the work was published?

If the work was published after the author died but before 1 January 1969, then copyright expires 50 years from the end of the year in which the work was published. If the author died on or after 1 January 1969 then the 70-year rule applies as in other cases (but see Section 4.103 for non-EEA authors).

Compilations and periodicals

4.107   What about works made up of contributions by several people?

The copyright expires separately for each contribution. So the copyright in papers in a collection of conference proceedings all expire at different times, depending on when each contributor dies. However, the copyright in the typography expires 25 years after the end of publication (see Sections 4.88 and following on typographical arrangement).

4.108   When does the copyright in a periodical issue run out?

The copyright in each article runs out 70 years after the death of the author (as for any other published literary work), but the copyright in the periodical issue as a whole (the typography) expires 25 years after publication. If the periodical was published outside the EEA and none of the authors is an EEA national, then copyright lasts for only as long as the country of publication provides.

4.109   Supposing the work contains illustrations by someone other than the author?

The copyright in the text and in the illustrations are separate.

Example: The text of the Pooh Bear stories was written by A. A. Milne, who died in 1956 (so copyright expires in 2026), but the illustrations were drawn by E. H. Shepard, who died in 1976 (so copyright expires in 2046).

Unpublished works

4.110   What if the work is unpublished?

The situation may sound complicated. If the author died before 1 January 1969, was a national of an EEA state and the work was unpublished at that time, copyright expires on 31 December 2039. If the author died on or after 1 January 1969, the work is protected for 70 years from the end of the year in which the author dies. If the author is not a national of an EEA state then copyright expires at the end of the term of protection which the author's national laws give.

Example: Author died on 22 November 1955. Copyright expires 31 December 2039. Author died on 3 December 1990. Copyright expires 31 December 2060 (death + 70 years). Note that the government carried out a consultation on simplifying these rules in 2015 but decided not to make any changes.

4.111   What if the author is still alive?

Copyright will last until 70 years after the end of the year in which the author dies, just like a published work, or, if from outside the EEA, the length of time the author's own nation gives.

4.112   Does this mean that all unpublished works cannot be used by anyone until 2039?

No. If the work was held by the library before 1 August 1989 and the author was already dead, then these documents can be copied, even with a view to publication, provided that the author has been dead for 50 years and the document is at least 100 years old. Note that copying is allowed 'with a view to publication' – the library or archive does not authorise publication. The law says that the work may be published if the publisher does not know the name and address of the copyright owner but it would be unwise to go ahead and publish if it was clear the copyright owner could easily be found – for example, if they were letters from a well-known politician or celebrity. In addition the library may make a copy of an orphan work for any of the following purposes without infringing copyright: making the orphan work available to the public; reproducing the orphan work for the purposes of digitisation, indexing, cataloguing, preservation or restoration.

Example: Author wrote a poem in 1875 and died in 1910. The poem could be copied after 31 December 1975. Note, however, that 'view to publication' does not mean they can be published – only copied in preparation for plans to seek permission to publish.

4.113   What about anonymous or pseudonymous works?

Unpublished anonymous or pseudonymous works are protected for 70 years from the end of the year in which they are created, or 70 years from first being made available to the public. However, where a work was created before 1 August 1989 copyright protection must last until 2039 regardless of the assumed date of creation. Despite this, if it is reasonable to assume the author has been dead for 70 years, then the work can be treated as out of copyright. Note that the government carried out a consultation on simplifying these rules in 2015 but decided not to make any changes.

4.114   What happens once anonymous or pseudonymous works are published?

They are protected for 70 years from the end of the year in which they were published. This includes not only publishing but public performance or broadcasting.

4.115 Supposing it is not possible to judge when a document was created?

There are special provisions for this situation. Where it is not possible by reasonable inquiry to find the identity of the author, and it is reasonable to suppose the copyright has expired, then the work may be treated as out of copyright.

4.116 What constitutes 'reasonable'?

This is not defined. Common sense and professional judgement are needed to make a guesstimate as to when a work might have been written. One learned judge said that 'what is reasonable is what seems reasonable to the man on the Clapham omnibus'.

4.117 How is the length of copyright worked out if there are several authors?

A work is considered of joint authorship if it is not possible to tell which author wrote which part. If different elements are attributed to different authors then each element is treated as a separate copyright work. So a book by Jones and Brown is joint authorship unless it identifies some specific chapters by Jones and some by Brown. The exception is a musical work with words (see below). Where a work has joint authorship, copyright lasts until 70 years after the end of the year in which the last author dies. If at least one of the authors is known, then any unknown ones are disregarded. Where some authors are EEA nationals and others are not, the work is treated as qualifying for the EEA term of protection (death + 70 years) or death of the last author to die if this gives a longer term of protection.

Example: A work has three authors; two are EEA nationals and one is not. The two EEA nationals die in 1955 and 1960 respectively, giving a term of protection until 2030, but the third, non-EEA author, whose country gives 50 years protection, does not die until 1995, giving protection until 2045.

4.118 What about works made up of words and music?

When a work is made up of words and music which were created in order to be used together then these are called works of co-authorship. In this case copyright in the whole work expires 70 (or 50 if the country of origin gives only 50) years from the end of the year in which the last of the collaborators dies.

Crown and Parliamentary copyright

4.119   How long does Crown copyright last?

Crown copyright in a literary, dramatic or musical work lasts for 125 years from the year in which the work was created or 50 years from the year in which it was first commercially published, provided this happens within 75 years of the year of creation. In other words, 125 years is the maximum.

Example: A report is prepared in 1930. Its copyright will run out in 2055. But if it is published commercially, say, in 1960, then the copyright runs out in 2010.

4.120   What if the author in the example did not die until 1970?

It makes no difference. The length of Crown copyright is linked to the date of creation or date of publication, not the human being responsible for creating the work.

4.121   Supposing some papers were not released because of the 'Thirty Year Rule' and were secret until then?

This makes no difference. Copyright runs from the year in which the work was created.

4.122   How long does Parliamentary copyright last?

It lasts for 50 years from the year in which the work was created.

4.123   Are the publications of other governments protected in the same way?

No. Publications of other governments are protected as if they were ordinary commercial publications in the UK. In the case of the USA, the US government claims no copyright in its own publications within the USA and it would seem unlikely that they should be protected in the UK in a way that they are not in the USA. So it is generally assumed that United States Government Printing Office (USGPO) publications are not protected by copyright.

Typographical copyright

4.124   How long does typographical copyright last?

Typographical copyright lasts for 25 years from the end of the year in which the work is published.

4.125   When does the copyright on a published work actually expire?

There are two dates. One, usually the earlier, will be the typographical one which runs out 25 years after first publication. However, the author's copyright continues until 70 (or 50) years after death. So the copyright in a book runs out in two stages. This does nothing to help people who want to copy it within that 25-year period. However, it allows republication by another publisher if the author has retained the copyright and not assigned it exclusively to the first publisher.

4.126   Does this mean that every time a book is reprinted the copyright begins again?

No. If the reprint is simply a reproduction of the original typographical arrangement, no new copyright comes into force.

4.127   Supposing it is a new layout of the book?

Then typographical copyright subsists in that particular edition.

4.128   What if it is the same typesetting but a long new introduction has been written?

There will be a new copyright in the new introduction, owned originally by the author of that introduction. The publisher can claim copyright in the whole work (introduction and text together) but the original text will only be a reproduction of an earlier text and is covered only for the time that typographical copyright lasts.

Example: *The Best of Saki* introduced by Tom Sharpe, London, Pan Books, 10th impression 1983, first published 1976. Initially it looks anonymous but Saki is the pen name of Hector Hugo Munro, killed in action 1916. So copyright in the stories expired in 1966 (author's death + 50 years as the rule was then). The publisher published in 1976 so no permission is needed as the stories are out of copyright. Typography was set up in 1976 so copyright in that expired in 2001 (25 years). The 10th impression in 1983 is not new typography so no new copyright exists. However, the introduction is by Tom Sharpe, who did not die until 2013, so that element only of the book is still in copyright until 2083 (author's death + 70 years).

Exceptions to copyright owners' rights

Copying materials

4.129   Can any copying at all be carried out without permission?

The law makes certain exceptions to the exclusive rights which owners enjoy over their works. The most important for libraries are certain rights to copy and lend copyright works.

4.130   For what purposes can a copyright work be used without the owner's consent?

There are several reasons given in the law. The most commonly claimed and most frequently quoted is fair dealing. But the following paragraphs describe the different situations when material can be copied.

Copying for private use

4.131   Can a work be copied for private use?

Note that the government introduced a right to make copies of whole works for private use provided the person making the copy owned that copy. This was struck down by the courts and does not now exist.

Fair dealing

4.132   What is fair dealing?

The concept of fair dealing has never been defined. The idea behind it seems to be that there may be good reasons for using something so long as the use does not harm the copyright owner or author but nevertheless benefits either the individual or society generally.

4.133   Does fair dealing just mean copying a work?

No. It includes copying but also using material in presentations, sound recordings, broadcasts, films and websites.

4.134   Does fair dealing apply to all copyright works?

Yes, but the different types of fair dealing apply differently to different classes of material. This section deals with literary, dramatic and musical works. For other works see the relevant sections. It applies to literary, dramatic and musical works for non-commercial research and private study and also for news reporting, criticism, review and quotations.

4.135   How much of a work can be copied under fair dealing?

Nobody knows for certain – it is a matter of individual judgement in each case.

What is clear is that until a substantial part of a work is copied, there can be no infringement, so defences such as fair dealing are not needed. But 'substantial' is not defined either and can be a very small part of a work. (See Section 3.35 for more detail.)

4.136 Does copying just mean photocopying?

No. The copying can be done using any techniques as the law does not specify the method of copying. See Section 4.33. So it also includes using a digital camera or mobile phone as well as a scanner.

4.137 Is there no guidance at all as to what fair dealing actually is?

In the law, no. Various guidelines have been issued in the past but they are guidelines only and are not part of the law, so they could be challenged by individual copyright owners.

4.138 How can anyone judge if copying something is 'fair'?

Look at the amount to be copied in conjunction with the reason for making the copy. No concrete examples can be given but consider the following: copying a whole work for non-commercial purposes, which has long been out of print and unavailable, might be 'fair', but copying the same work just to save buying a copy is obviously not.

4.139 What are the justifications for fair dealing?

The law recognises several. The one most commonly cited in libraries is copying for non-commercial research or private study. The other purposes are reporting current events and also criticism, review and quotation. This last exception also covers caricature, parody and pastiche.

Research for a non-commercial purpose or private study
4.140 What constitutes 'research'?

The word is not defined in law but the court would probably give it its natural meaning.

4.141 What does 'non-commercial' mean?

The law does not say and it must be up to each individual to decide if the copying is fair and for a non-commercial purpose. Any use that brings financial benefit to the person making the copy will certainly be commercial and therefore excluded.

4.142   Are there any other restrictions?

Yes. When copying something for non-commercial research purposes the source must be acknowledged.

4.143   What can be done for someone who does want a copy for commercial purposes?

The copying must be carried out with the permission of the copyright owner. Usually this is done through a licence offered by the appropriate licensing agency (see Section 10), but, if none of the licences mentioned there apply, then permission must be sought directly from the copyright owner. This may be the author or the publisher, depending on the circumstances.

4.144   Is private study limited to students?

Not at all, if, by 'student' is meant someone in an academic institution. Anyone undertaking training or education of any kind, including leisure courses such as evening classes in hobbies or holiday languages, can reasonably claim fair dealing as a 'student'. But to do this the copying must be done by the student personally and not on behalf of the student.

4.145   Can this be done by someone in industry and commerce?

This would be difficult to justify, as the definition of private study now specifically excludes 'any study which is directly or indirectly for a commercial purpose'. Again, the user will need to make this judgement for each copy made for private study purposes.

4.146   Why private study?

Private study is thought of as being undertaken alone. Therefore multiple copying for classroom use cannot be private study and is provided for separately under educational copying (see below).

4.147   Does fair dealing allow the making of more than one copy?

If the student or researcher does the copying themselves it might be possible to make more than one copy.

   Example: Suppose a student has to go on a geography field trip. Two copies of a small portion of a map may be needed – one for use in the field (where it may get muddy or torn) and the other for the file relating to the project. If two copies are made they must be for the personal use only of the person who made them. But this is merely an opinion.

4.148 **Supposing the student wants a copy for personal use and one for a friend?**

Not allowed! If any copying is done on behalf of someone else then the person making the copy must not make it if they know that this will result in a copy of substantially the same material being supplied to more than one person at substantially the same time and for substantially the same purpose. But always remember that your institution may have a licence, which would allow this.

Example: Three students may make for themselves one copy each of, say, a journal article, for use in a lecture or project. But if one makes copies for personal use and copies for the two friends then this is an infringement.

4.149 **What do all these instances of 'substantially' mean?**

They are not defined but it would seem likely that someone copying pages 9–14 for themselves and pages 10–16 for a friend or colleague would have copied 'substantially the same material' and that this copying, if done on Monday and Wednesday of the same week for use in the same tutorial or related experiments at the laboratory bench, would constitute copying at substantially the same time and for substantially the same purpose.

4.150 **What about self-service machines?**

Although these are not dealt with specifically, the Act differentiates between copies made by students or researchers themselves and those made for them by other people. Although nothing is said in this context about providing equipment that might be used for infringing purposes, it is clear from another part of the Act that it is not an offence to possess equipment that can be used for breach of copyright, as opposed to equipment which can be used only for breach of copyright. It would be foolish for any librarian deliberately to turn a blind eye to copying which was beyond the law, and a suitable notice giving details of what is and is not allowed should be displayed (contact CILIP for a suggested text), but whether a librarian could actually be held responsible is open to doubt. Any notice should refer to the CDPA and its restrictions. These should also be mentioned in any publicity for the library's services and any user education courses which are offered. Generally librarians are expected to use their best endeavours to ensure that equipment in their care is not used for infringements of copyright.

4.151   What if the person asks the librarian to do the copying for them?

This situation is dealt with specifically by the Copyright Act and copying by libraries is dealt with in detail in Sections 4.192 and following.

4.152   What about downloading from databases, either online or on CD-ROM?

See Section 9 for detailed guidance.

Text and data mining

4.153   If material contains useful data or figures can these be copied and used in further research?

Yes. If the user needs to copy a work so that they can make a computational analysis of data or text in the document, then the copying is permitted.

4.154   Are there any special rules?

There are four requirements:

- The user must have lawful access to the document.
- The use must be for research of a non-commercial purpose.
- The source of the information must be acknowledged unless this is not possible.
- The copy must not be passed to any other person without the copyright owner's permission.
  This exception cannot be overruled by any contractual agreement.

Criticism, review and quotation

4.155   Can these exceptions be used for any type of criticism or quotation?

The law says that you may use a copyright work for the purposes of criticism, review, quotation, caricature, parody or pastiche.

4.156   Are these terms defined?

There is no definition of any of them. The European court has said that parody must be both humorous and satirical but who decides what is and what is not humorous is another matter! As it is unlikely that libraries and similar bodies will be much involved in caricature, parody or pastiche these topics will not be dealt with specifically.

4.157 Are there restrictions on which types of work can be quoted?

No. This exception applies to all forms of work.

Criticism

4.158 Can libraries claim they use material for criticism or review?

An important exception for librarians of all kinds is criticism or review. It is allowed to quote parts of a work when writing critical essays or reviews such as book reviews or comparisons of different authors' works in academic research.

4.159 How much can be quoted?

That is open to individual judgement, but you must limit the amount quoted to no more than is necessary for the specific purpose for which the quotation is required. The source of the quotations must be given, for example, the full bibliographic reference in a review is essential, as the reviewer may be encouraging the reader to buy a copy! The same is true if a criticism is being written of the writings of a single author. Libraries that prepare their own reviews for the general public or in the form of information bulletins for researchers should note the conditions under which, and to what extent, they can quote the works mentioned.

4.160 Are there any rules to be observed?

Yes. The work quoted must have been made available to the public and the source of the quotation must be acknowledged, because if the work has not been made available, then quoting it in a review would result in part of it being published. The amount used must also be considered fair dealing.

4.161 What does 'made available to the public' mean?

In the context of using material for the purpose of criticism the meaning includes:

- issuing copies to the public
- making the work available by means of an electronic retrieval system
- renting out or lending copies of the work to the public

- performing, exhibiting, playing or showing of the work in public
- communicating the work to the public.

4.162 Does this review idea extend to news bulletins?

No. See 'Reporting current events' below.

Quotation

4.163 If someone writes an article or a book and wants to quote something relevant to the subject from another person's work, is this allowed?

Yes (and it used not to be specifically permitted until 2014!). The amount quoted must, once again, be no more than is necessary for the purpose for which it is quoted.

Reporting current events

4.164 What is a current event?

A current event is something defined less by time than by current interest. It can be something which happened yesterday or today, but equally it might be something that happened several years ago but which has become a matter of interest to the public now.

4.165 Can any material be used?

Any work can be used except a photograph.

4.166 Supposing the news items that are needed include a photograph?

Clearly the law is intended to protect the very considerable investment in photography made by newspapers and without this exception any evening paper could use the photographs of any morning one for its news story. In theory this also applies to internal and local news bulletins made from clippings but it is very difficult to exclude a photograph in the middle of a piece of news text. Technically it should be blacked out. This can more easily be achieved by scanning the document and then editing out the illustration(s). The alternative is to retype the necessary text. But see Section 10 for possible copying under licence from the Newspaper Licensing Agency (NLA) or the Copyright Licensing Agency (CLA).

4.167 Supposing the news bulletin is prepared and displayed electronically?

The same rules apply as for a clippings service.

4.168 Are there any other restrictions?

Yes, the source of the work quoted must be acknowledged unless this is not possible for reasons of practicality or otherwise.

4.169 What does that mean?

Presumably it means you must acknowledge the source if you can find it out.

Educational copying

See also Section 10 on licences.

4.170 Are the amounts which may be copied for educational copying just as vague as in fair dealing?

No, the rules are quite different.

4.171 What is the difference between copying for educational purposes and copying for private study?

Private study does not mean for classroom use. Educational copying is for classroom use. All librarians in any organisation where teaching takes place should be aware of what is allowed, as the materials in their care are frequently used for educational purposes. This is also true for public libraries, which are used for project work. Educational copying exceptions do not apply to training in commercial or industrial companies.

4.172 Can a teacher or student copy anything for use in the classroom?

Yes. The purpose must be to illustrate the teaching being given and this exception does not include making multiple copies for classroom use. The copying must be done by the person giving or receiving instruction or preparing for giving or receiving instruction. The purpose must be non-commercial educational instruction and the source must be acknowledged. This exception cannot be overridden by any contractual agreement.

4.173   Does instruction apply only to schools and universities?

No, but the instruction must be for a non-commercial purpose. So training and education in a commercial company is excluded but purely internal training in, say, a military organisation may well be included.

4.174   Can any amount be copied?

If it has been made available to the public then the copying must be fair. In other words, so much of a work must not be copied that it becomes unnecessary to buy a copy or copies of the work for teaching purposes, or it is done to avoid being copied under the CLA licence (see Section 10).

4.175   What does 'made available to the public' mean?

It has the same definition as for criticism. See Section 4.161.

4.176   What about copying for examinations?

Any work may be copied for setting an examination question, communicating the question to the students or answering the question, but the amount copied must be fair to the copyright owner and whole works cannot be copied. In addition the source must be acknowledged in the question (but not necessarily the answer!).

4.177   What if a student needs to include some copyright material in a thesis or dissertation for a degree?

This would seem to be covered in providing the answers to an examination. If the thesis is subsequently copied for other purposes, or published, then clearance would be needed from the copyright owner.

4.178   What happens if several children come into the public library, all asking for copies of the same thing for their project?

Only one copy can be provided. It is unclear at what age a child could provide the necessary declaration (see Section 4.224) as a legal minor. However, although schools operated by local authorities usually have a licence to copy necessary materials, such licences may allow copying only from books and magazines in the school's own collection and not those held by other libraries. Teachers should check with the CLA or NLA terms as appropriate.

4.179   What about including some copyright material in collections put together by teachers?

There are special rules governing this which should be known by the teacher or publisher and not worry the librarian too much. Section 33 of the Act sets out the limits for this sort of publishing, for which librarians are sometimes asked to provide the original material to copy.

4.180   What about using material in virtual learning environments?

See Section 11.52 for information about virtual learning environments (VLEs).

Copying by or for educational establishments

4.181   What counts as an educational establishment?

An educational establishment is defined as:

- any school
- any university allowed to award degrees under Act of Parliament or royal charter
- any institution empowered to offer further or higher education under the Education (Scotland) Act 1980, the Education and Libraries (Northern Ireland) Order 1986 or the Education Reform Act 1988 (see SI 2005/223 for exact details)
- any theological college.

4.182   Can anyone else exercise these privileges?

Yes, any person can make the copy provided the instruction is for a non-commercial purpose.

4.183   Multiple copying is not allowed, so what can be done for teachers who need multiple copies of parts of works to use for instruction?

The Act allows two ways forward. If a licence can be obtained (see Section 10) then that should be taken out and the conditions followed. If no licence is obtainable the law permits the copying of up to 5% of a work within a 12-month period. These allowances cannot be claimed if the person doing the copying knows or ought to know of a licensing scheme. Note that any licence cannot restrict copying to levels below what the law permits.

4.184   Can this copying be done on behalf of the teacher or student by someone else?

Yes, but the conditions of any contract or licence must be adhered to.

4.185   Do these exceptions apply to all materials?

No. Broadcasts are excluded, as are artistic works unless they are incorporated into another work. For example, a photograph cannot be copied unless it forms part of a journal article or chapter in a book.

4.186   Can material be made available in electronic form to students?

Yes. The law permits the making available through dedicated terminals electronic copies of works held by the educational establishment to individual members of the public.

4.187   Must these already be in electronic format?

No. The establishment may make a digital copy of a work and then make that copy available through dedicated terminals for the purposes of research or private study.

4.188   Does this exclude their use for commercial research?

Apparently not, as the law specifically says 'research' and does not mention non-commercial use.

4.189   Could an educational establishment digitise its entire collection of material for this purpose?

No. This would violate the concept behind exceptions, that they must be for a 'specific purpose'.

4.190   Are there any other conditions?

Yes. The work must have been acquired lawfully by the establishment and the making available must be done with regard to any contractual or licensing conditions under which it was made available to the establishment. Note that the terminals are for viewing by individual members of the public, so any form of group viewing is excluded. Terminals should be for access by one person at a time only.

4.191 What about students or staff who are located outside the campus or in other premises?

The electronic communication must be via a secure electronic network accessible only to the students and staff.

Libraries, archives, museums and galleries

4.192 Are there exceptions for libraries?

These exceptions are the most important limitation on owners' rights as far as librarians are concerned. The main user group mentioned in the Act is librarians and archivists. These terms include curators in museums and galleries as well. The special exceptions for libraries apply to all forms of works protected by copyright. Therefore any work protected by database right is not covered by these regulations. See Section 9 for details. These exceptions are often referred to as 'library privilege'. This is a useful shorthand term but is not a legal one. Note that the rules governing the exceptions apply where the librarian or archivist makes the copies on behalf of the user. Where users copy for themselves they claim fair dealing and not library privilege.

4.193 Are the terms 'library', 'archive', 'museum' and 'gallery' defined?

There are no definitions of what constitutes a library, archive, museum or gallery, but which ones qualify for library privileges is set out in the Act.

4.194 Do all libraries and so on qualify for the privileges given under the Act?

No. Only qualifying libraries qualify!

4.195 What constitutes a qualifying library, archive, museum or gallery?

Any library, archive, museum or gallery wishing to exercise the privileges set out in the following paragraphs must fulfil the following conditions:

- be publicly accessible, or
- be the library of an educational establishment and
- not be owned by a body which is conducted for profit or is part of a body conducted for profit.

4.196   What exactly is an educational establishment?

See Section 4.181 for the definition.

4.197   What does 'publicly accessible' mean?

There is no definition. It is definitely not linked to physical access by people with disabilities. Presumably it means any library which is accessible for consultation by a significant segment of the public.

4.198   What about libraries that are part of government establishments but are not open to the general public for security or other reasons?

Presumably it can be argued that they are accessible to a significant part of the public – most government departments and agencies and their employees. As such bodies need a performing rights licence for music on the premises, and this is deemed playing music to the public, they must be accessible to the public.

4.199   What about making materials available to readers through dedicated terminals?

The basic rules set out in 4.186 and following apply to libraries as they do to educational establishments.

Copying published literary, dramatic and musical works

4.200   What are qualifying libraries and so on allowed to do that is special?

Quite a lot, as described in the following paragraphs. First, they can supply copies of works to their users.

Copying for users – periodicals

4.201   What constitutes a periodical?

This is not defined. The word 'periodical' implies some concept of being issued at periods of time. Therefore monographs in series, technical report literature and publishers' series would probably not count as periodicals, as they are not linked to any timescale. A further problem could be newspapers. Although most librarians view newspapers as periodicals some dictionaries define the word 'periodical' as excluding newspapers!

4.202 **Is there a limit on how much of a work can be copied for a user?**

Yes. There are different limits for different kinds of material. In the case of a periodical, no user can be supplied with a copy of more than one article in the same periodical issue.

4.203 **Can the user have more than one copy of the same article?**

Not under the law. This must be done with the permission of the copyright owner. See Section 9 on licences.

4.204 **Supposing the volume of separate issues has been bound, how does this affect copying?**

The law is not specific but it seems likely that the interpretation would be that not more than one article could be copied from any one original periodical part as issued to the public.

4.205 **Supposing the article includes some drawings or photographs. Is it permitted to copy these as well?**

Yes. If an article is copied for someone, then it is permitted to copy any accompanying illustrations. Accompanying is an important word. If the article is in, say, an art journal and is supplemented by high-quality plates of paintings just to further illustrate the artist's work, these may not be copied unless they are intrinsic to the understanding of the text. But they might be copied if only a reasonable part of them is copied. See Section 5 on copying artistic works.

4.206 **What counts as an 'article'?**

Unfortunately this term is defined only in very general terms. An article, in the context of an article in a periodical, means an item of any description.

4.207 **Does this include things like advertisements, the title page, contents page or index?**

Yes, so the user should not really be supplied with an article from an issue as well as the contents page.

4.208 **What about making copies of contents pages and circulating them for information among staff?**

This is not allowed. First, it is multiple copying; second, the library cannot make copies for people unless they sign a declaration form first. However, as the contents page is a statement of a series of facts (which are not in themselves covered by copyright) there seems no reason why the contents page cannot be re-typed, avoiding copying the typographical arrangement. If the journal is electronic then a link could be provided to the contents page for individuals to look through it for themselves.

4.209   Is copying title pages not allowed at all?

Only as described above. Alternatively, it is a good idea to write to the publishers concerned and ask if they will permit this. Most say they will, as it is good advertising for their journals, but some take the view that it could encourage related copying (more than one copy requested by different people at the same time for the same purpose).

4.210   Supposing the user wants two articles from the same issue?

Only one can be provided. However, it might be possible for the user to claim fair dealing if the user borrowed the periodical issue and made the copies personally. This would then require a fair dealing defence (see Sections 4.130 onwards). An alternative would be to copy under a licence. See Section 10.

4.211   If a publisher charges a higher rate for a library subscription to a periodical, can more copying be done?

No, unless the publisher has specifically stated this in the publicity, catalogues or in a specific letter to the library.

4.212   Can articles be copied from newspapers?

Yes. Whether the rules for copying from monographs or periodicals apply is slightly doubtful. Note also there is the NLA (see Section 10).

4.213   But to copy one article from a newspaper often involves incidentally copying another, or at least part of another. What is the position then?

Technically only the article actually required can be copied. To be perfectly correct all other parts of the page should be blacked out! But this would be incidental copying, really as an accident or done simply in the normal process of doing what is allowed. If a case were brought, it might be possible to argue, by analogy, incidental copying similar to that allowed for artistic works in photographs (see Section 5.25), but that is only an opinion.

4.214 Does the copying of an article extend to conference proceedings?

It depends on the nature of the conference publication. Many annual or more frequent conferences appear simply as 'Proceedings of the xth conference on....' and could be viewed as a serial. Others with no clear numbering, or with monographic titles, must be treated as books. If the conference is held regularly (annually is the most common) then it could be a periodical. A further test would be if the proceedings had an ISSN. Conferences which are merely numbered with no indication of the timescale in which they are held are most likely monographs (non-periodical publications).

4.215 What about technical reports in a numbered series?

Generally these must be treated as separate monographs.

4.216 Supposing the periodical issue consists of just one article?

The law specifically states that one article may be copied from a periodical issue. It seems clear that this allows the copying of an article if it constitutes the entire issue of a periodical although any other material in that issue, such as title page, advertisements or other ephemeral material, must not be copied.

4.217 What about individually tailored information services?

The arrangement whereby the librarian scans various information services for material that is considered relevant to the research of library users and then obtains copies of these items and passes them on to users without being asked for them is an infringement unless a licence has been obtained.

4.218 What can be done for researchers in this situation?

There is no reason why a librarian may not produce a current awareness bulletin from which staff select and request items they require, but they must ask for items and not have them sent gratuitously.

Copying for users – material other than periodicals

4.219 What about copying material that is not a periodical?

Only a reasonable proportion of a non-periodical work can be copied. The rules for copying material other than periodicals apply to all types of material – monographs, artistic works, sound recordings, films and broadcasts – but not to databases.

4.220   What exactly is a monograph?

The law does not use the word 'monograph' (or 'book' except in relation to PLR), but rather 'published edition other than an article in a periodical'.

4.221   What constitutes a 'reasonable' proportion?

This is not defined, but a general view from the publishing industry has been that '10% or a chapter' might be reasonable. Although this is not a legal definition it is a helpful guideline. It seems safe to assume that a reasonable proportion is larger than a substantial part because if less than a substantial part had been copied, there would be no need to claim any defence. Like substantial part and fair dealing, this is a matter of individual judgement.

4.222   Supposing a book consists mostly of photographs and plates?

Each item is a copyright item in its own right and must be treated as such. Libraries may copy artistic works (such as photographs and plates) on behalf of users (see Section 5). They may also copy illustrations that accompany the text requested.

Restrictions on copying for users

4.223   Can any librarian copy for someone under these conditions?

No. Only librarians working in qualifying libraries may undertake this copying.

4.224   Are there other restrictions?

Yes. The librarian can copy an article from a periodical or part of a published work only in response to a written request that includes the name of the person making the request and the material that the person requires, and a declaration that:

- a copy has not previously been supplied by any library
- the copy will be used only for research for a non-commercial purpose or private study and that it will not be supplied to any other person
- to the best of the person's knowledge no other person with whom the person works or studies has made or intends to make at about the same time a request for substantially the same material for substantially the same purpose.

In addition, the librarian must not provide the copy if she or he is aware that the declaration is false in any substantial part.

4.225 **The term 'substantially' has turned up again. Is it defined in this part of the Act any better than in the other?**

No. The same uncertainty applies (see Sections 3.35–36).

4.226 **Can a user really be expected to make a statement about the intentions of other people?**

No, that is not what is being asked. Users say that to the best of their knowledge nobody else is going to ask for copies of substantially the same material. Thus the user can be in complete ignorance and truthfully sign the form.

4.227 **Does this declaration have to be made when the request is made?**

No. But it must be made before the copy is handed over. These two actions often coincide in smaller libraries but in large libraries or public libraries there is often a waiting time between the request and the arrival of the copy. It is perfectly in order to obtain the declaration at the time the request is made but it must be borne in mind that in some circumstances a copy may not be supplied but the original lent instead. In this case the declaration is superfluous. On the other hand the requester may not be aware that the request will be fulfilled by a photocopy, so it would be reasonable not to ask for a declaration until the document was handed over.

4.228 **What happens when requests are received by telephone or letter?**

The request can be processed but the copies cannot be handed over until the declaration form has been presented. This may well cause rather long correspondence but there is no easy way round this.

4.229 **Can the declaration be sent by fax?**

Yes.

4.230 **Can the declaration be made electronically rather than having to visit the library in person?**

Yes, the declaration must be in writing but the form of that writing is not specified.

4.231 **Must libraries charge for making copies for readers?**

No. This is no longer obligatory. If the library does charge, the amount must be calculated with reference to the cost attributed to making the copy.

4.232   What if something is required urgently?

You need to use ingenuity, but the law must be observed.

4.233   Is there a standard form in which this declaration must be made?

No. The content of the declaration is set out as above but the exact layout and text can be varied.

4.234   So, as long as these conditions are met, can any librarian copy for a user?

It is not so simple. The user must sign a declaration but, in addition, the librarian must be satisfied that the requirements of two or more people are not similar or related and that no person is furnished with:

- more than one copy
- more than one article from a periodical issue or more than a reasonable part of any other published work.

4.235   How can a librarian tell if the requirements of two or more users are 'similar'?

Similar is defined only in terms of substantially the same material at substantially the same time and for substantially the same purpose!

4.236   Is there really no guidance as to what these terms mean?

No. It is fairly easy to give examples of what would be regarded as substantial as in Section 4.149, but it is very difficult to say what would not be regarded as substantial in these terms.

4.237   How can a librarian tell if requirements are related?

This is a lot easier. Related is defined as 'if those persons receive instruction to which material is relevant at the same time and place'. This is to stop classroom copying by libraries in educational establishments.

4.238   Supposing they are two students at a university requiring the copies for totally different courses?

This does not seem to matter. They still require them for substantially the same purpose and they are receiving instruction in the same place, although this might not apply if two lecturers asked for the same material for totally different courses and on different campuses.

4.239   Can the librarian rely on the user's honesty when providing the declaration form?

Basically yes, in respect of the purposes for which the copy is required, but certain measures to ensure the law is complied with must also be in place.

4.240   Supposing the user provides a declaration and it turns out to be untrue?

Librarians cannot be expected to know the inner motives of their users and the law recognises this. The librarian may rely on a signed declaration from the reader as to the purpose for which the copy is required and the truthfulness of the statement that a copy has not been supplied by another librarian previously.

4.241   Then who is liable if the user provides a false declaration?

The law specifies that it is the user who would be guilty as if they had made the copy themselves.

4.242   How can a librarian know that a copy has not been obtained from another library?

That is not possible. But the declaration which the user provides specifically states that the user has not been supplied with a copy by you or any other librarian.

4.243   Can the user give the copy to someone else?

No. The law now states that the copy will not be supplied to any other person.

4.244   What happens if the user no longer requires the copy and subsequently gives these copies back to the library?

The user has agreed the copy will not be supplied to anyone else so giving it to the library (or anyone else) is not an option.

4.245   Would it be best to destroy such copies?

Not necessarily. The user is entitled to keep the copy and may add it to files of other papers. These are often then deposited in an appropriate department of the institution or company. A suitable registry would need to be used for depositing such material, but see the previous paragraph.

4.246 **If a user gives the copy to someone else, can a user have another from the library?**

No, and the copy should not have been supplied to anyone else.

4.247 **Supposing a user genuinely lost the previous copy?**

The librarian cannot legally supply another. Readers should not be so careless! However, there seems to be nothing to stop readers borrowing the item and making a further copy for their private use. In this case, the copying would fall outside the provisions for libraries and become fair dealing.

4.248 **What is the position if a second user also genuinely asks for the same material as the first, equally ignorant of the request by the first person?**

If the librarian is aware of this, the second person cannot be supplied with a copy.

4.249 **Isn't that rather unfair on the second user?**

Perhaps so. But the idea is that a user should share the first person's copy. Presumably sharing would not be considered to be supplying. 'You can look at this copy with me but you can't have it to keep.'

4.250 **Do all these references to the 'librarian' really mean only the person in charge of the library?**

No. The law says that references to the librarian include a person acting on behalf of the librarian, archivist or curator.

4.251 **Can any librarian make a copy for any member of the public?**

No. Only staff from qualifying libraries can do this and the declaration form must always be provided to ensure the conditions for making the copy are met.

4.252 **Must all library users pay?**

There is no obligation to charge. See Section 4.231.

4.253 **Is the amount specified?**

No, but the way it is calculated is. See Section 4.231.

4.254 **Is photocopying subject to value added tax?**

Yes, although the amounts on individual copies may be so small that a per-page charge, which is calculated to include the value added tax (VAT), is probably the most practicable way to collect this.

4.255 Can material held in the library's collection be made available in electronic form to the public without infringing copyright?

Yes, under specific conditions. The conditions are that:

- the work (or a copy of it) has been lawfully acquired
- the work is communicated via a dedicated terminal on the premises
- the purpose of communicating the work must be for research or private study
- communication must be in compliance with any purchasing or licensing terms to which the work is subject.

Again, terminals must be accessible to individuals, not for group viewing.

4.256 What about viewing the material for commercial research purposes?

The law makes no mention in this area of the research being for non-commercial purposes only.

Interlibrary supply

4.257 What does the term 'interlibrary supply' actually mean?

The term 'supply' has been used because it is important to distinguish between lending and copying for interlibrary purposes. For lending between libraries see Sections 4.65 and following. Copies supplied between libraries are often referred to as 'interlibrary loans' but they are actually copies supplied for retention. It is also important to distinguish between interlibrary copying, which is intended for one library to supply copies for the collection of another library, and copying for individuals who have made their request to their own library, which does not hold the material required and which has therefore transmitted the request to another library. The law makes provision for interlibrary copying but copying by one library for users of another library must be treated as a two-stage process.

Interlibrary copying for use by individuals

4.258   What about supplying copies through interlibrary arrangements for individual users?

Either the library that receives the original request must send it on to another library with an appropriate declaration form (see Sections 4.224 and following), or the library which receives the request must have a clear agreement with the library to which the request is sent that the first library will collect and retain a declaration form on behalf of the second library, which made the copy. Otherwise the library making the copy has no proof that the copy was made legally.

Example: A researcher in Swatville University asks the librarian for a copy of an article from a periodical which Swatville University Library does not take but which is taken by Sometown University. The librarian of Swatville University applies to Sometown University, acting simply as the letterbox for the researcher, who is entitled to ask for copies from Sometown University under the library provisions. The librarian of Swatville University must be aware that Sometown University Library sees the librarian as acting as their agent to handle requests from individuals, which are to be passed to Sometown University. So either Swatville sends the request with a user declaration form or there is a proper agreement between Sometown and Swatville that requests sent to Sometown by Swatville will have had a declaration form completed and kept by Swatville University Library.

Interlibrary copying for library collections

4.259   What about supplying copies of works in various formats for library collections?

This is allowed for certain libraries only.

4.260   Which libraries can supply copies, then?

Any library in the UK can make and supply copies of material in its collection.

4.261   What about receiving copies?

Only qualifying libraries may request and receive copies for their collections.

4.262   What is a qualifying library?

See Section 4.181 for the definition of an educational establishment and 4.195 for the definition of a qualifying library.

4.263 **What about private libraries?**

Some private libraries could say they are conducted for profit and in that case they cannot qualify, but others are charitable in status and again it will depend on the nature of the charity.

4.264 **Are the rules for libraries that can supply copies different?**

Yes. Any library (whether conducted for profit or not) can supply a copy through interlibrary arrangements but not all libraries can receive a copy.

4.265 **Can anything be copied by qualifying libraries?**

No. There are restrictions on periodical articles and other works.

4.266 **What are the restrictions?**

No library may be supplied with more than one copy of any material. Except in the case of periodical articles, no library may be supplied with a copy of part or all of a work unless that library makes a formal request and the librarian making the copy does not know, and could not reasonably find out, the name and address of someone entitled to authorise the making of the copy.

4.267 **What does 'reasonably find out' mean?**

This is not defined but it should be remembered that as the library which is being asked to make the copy must hold the material it is possible that the requesting library could obtain the required information from the supplying library, and even more likely that the supplying library could find this out anyway. However, if the material is published by a company now out of business or in a remote corner of the world, and the publisher does not reply to correspondence, then the copies can be made. The government has issued guidelines for trying to find copyright owners in connection with orphan works, so these could be a useful basis for trying to find the copyright owner in these circumstances.

4.268 **Who is the person entitled to authorise the making of the copy?**

As the requirement is to make a copy of all or a substantial part of the work, the publisher is probably the only person who can authorise the making of such a copy, as publishers usually own the copyright in the total publication (as against authors, who own the content of the text, illustrators who own rights in their work, and so on). However, modern publishing contracts are usually for fixed, often short, terms, and so many rights in individual parts of the monograph may have reverted to the author. Even so, the publisher still owns the typographical copyright.

4.269 Is a qualifying library allowed to keep the copies and add them to stock?

Yes. This is one way that the problem of two people requiring the same material can be overcome. Reader A borrows the photocopy and returns it. Reader B then borrows it in the same way as she or he borrows any other library materials.

4.270 What if a copy is lost or destroyed?

On the face of it, a second copy could not possibly be asked for, as qualifying libraries may only request one copy and there is no time limit on this. However, it is a nice point that, if the photocopy had been placed in the permanent collection then the library might be able to request a replacement at some distant date, as the first photocopy is legitimate and can be regarded as part of the permanent collection. See Section 4.278.

4.271 Can the library subsequently dispose of the copy to another library?

It seems probable that this can be done only to another qualifying library, which did not already have a copy of the material in question.

4.272 Suppose the library sold off its collection. What should happen to the photocopies?

The copies cannot be sold as this would be dealing in them. The best that could be done is that they could be donated to another library.

4.273 Must libraries pay for interlibrary copying?

No, but the sum charged must be calculated with consideration for the actual cost of supplying the copy.

4.274 Does interlibrary copying attract VAT?

Yes, just as copying for individuals does.

4.275 How can a library that is not a qualifying library obtain a photocopy on interlibrary loan?

Libraries that are not qualifying libraries may not request material from other libraries for their collections but only for individuals for non-commercial purposes.

4.276 Can the non-qualifying library keep the copy?

No.

Copying for preservation

4.277 Can any library copy for preservation purposes?

No. They must be qualifying libraries.

4.278 Can qualifying libraries or archives copy their own materials under the conditions listed below?

Yes, so long as the conditions stipulated are fulfilled.

4.279 Can anything in a qualifying library be copied?

No. First, material has to be in the permanent collection of the library or archive. Therefore it is not allowed to borrow a document from somewhere else, put it into the collection temporarily, copy it and then return it to the original owner. This is particularly important for collections which are deposited for limited periods (e.g. the lifetime of the owner). It is also important for galleries and museums that borrow exhibits from elsewhere: they cannot make copies under this provision, as the material is not in the permanent collection. Second, the material has to be in the permanent collection and available only for reference on the premises, or part of the collection not accessible to the public or for loan only to other libraries. Third, it must not be reasonably practicable for the librarian or archivist to purchase a copy.

4.280 Is it permitted to make more than one copy for preservation?

This seems unlikely. The Act says 'a copy' may be made.

4.281 Must the copy be paper or can the preservation copy be in digital form?

As the Act defines copying as including making electronic copies (see Sections 4.31–35), there seems no reason why a preservation copy cannot be digital.

Copying for replacement of lost items

4.282 **Sometimes materials in the permanent reference collection are lost, damaged or destroyed. Can copies of this material be obtained from other libraries?**

Theft, careless use and fire are all examples of how this might happen. In these circumstances replacement copies can be obtained from other libraries.

4.283 **Which libraries can supply replacements?**

Any library or archive in the UK can supply copies for preservation and replacement; any qualifying library or any archive can request and receive replacement copies.

4.284 **For exactly which reasons can material be copied for replacement?**

The law allows copying in order to replace an item in the permanent collection, for reference purposes, and to replace material in another library which has been lost, damaged or destroyed. Clearly a library cannot replace material in its own collection in this way since, if it is lost or destroyed, it is not there to copy!

4.285 **Can one library or archive copy for another?**

Yes. The item being replaced must be used for the same purposes and under the same circumstances and copies made for preservation (see Section 4.277).

4.286 **What about books or periodicals in general lending collections which are falling apart or are lost?**

These cannot qualify for copying under these special regulations.

4.287 **Can the supplying library make a charge for supplying the copy?**

Yes, but if they do then the cost must be calculated with reference to the actual cost of supplying the copy. There is no obligation to charge.

4.288 **Could a qualifying library obtain a copy of a work from a library if the work was in the general lending collection of the supplying library or archive?**

Yes, provided the copy being made was for use only in the way described above.

4.289 Can these special provisions be overridden by a contract or licence?

No. The law specifies that any such clause in a contract is null and void.

Copying unpublished works

4.290 Can unpublished materials in a library be copied for users?

Yes, under certain conditions.

4.291 What are the conditions?

First, the work has not been published before the document was deposited. Second, copying may not take place if the copyright owner has prohibited this.

Example: Edward Gotrip writes a novel in the hope he will become famous and deposits the manuscript with the local public library. Subsequently it is published. The public library is entitled to copy the manuscript even though the text has become a published novel. However, Una Suming has her book published and then, having become famous, deposits the manuscript with the local public library, but no copying of it is allowed.

4.292 Can the librarian plead ignorance of the fact that the copyright owner had prohibited copying?

Not really. The law says that copies may not be made when the copyright owner has prohibited this and the librarian or archivist knows, or ought to know, that this is the case. Therefore it is sensible to keep a register of deposited unpublished material with notes on any items which the copyright owner has prohibited the library or archive from copying.

4.293 Can whole works be copied, or only parts?

The law allows copying of the whole of an unpublished document.

4.294 Can unpublished works be copied for anyone?

Yes, on condition that the reader provides a declaration to say that the documents are required only for non-commercial research or private study; a copy has not previously been supplied to the reader; and that the documents were not published before they were deposited. The declaration must also contain the name of the person requesting the copy and details of the document requested.

4.295   Do users have to pay?

No. But if a charge is made the cost must be calculated with consideration for the actual cost of making the copy.

4.296   Do the restrictions on not supplying copies to more than one person for substantially the same purpose at substantially the same time apply?

No, these restrictions are not laid down for unpublished works.

4.297   Is there a standard declaration form as for published materials?

No, but the contents of such a declaration are set out in the Act as outlined above.

4.298   Can copies be supplied from one archive to another?

No, except for the purposes of replacement because of loss, damage or destruction. As much unpublished material (e.g. manuscripts) is unique, this situation will not arise very often.

4.299   Can these provisions for unpublished works be overridden by contract or licence?

No exception is made for them in the legislation, partly because this situation is dealt with by the requirement that the copyright owner has not prohibited copying and the fact that there are no licences for copying unpublished material.

Abstracts

4.300   Does the abstract that goes with a journal article have a separate copyright?

Yes. It is a distinct work, which can stand alone – otherwise it is not really an abstract.

4.301   Can any abstract be copied?

Yes, but not those which are prepared specifically for abstracting services such as *Chemical Abstracts*. The law says abstracts that accompany articles on scientific or technical subjects may be copied, provided there is no licensing scheme, but just what 'scientific' or 'technical' means is open for discussion.

4.302   Can the abstract be copied with the article?

Yes. The law states that such abstracts can be copied freely unless there is a licensing scheme which covers them, in which case you must belong to the scheme to copy the abstracts. So far no such scheme has been devised.

4.303   How about writing abstracts for information services?

It is quite in order to prepare abstracts from scratch by summarising the article concerned using skill and knowledge to read the article and present the information in a different form. You should not use actual text from the original article. Once written, the copyright belongs to the abstractor or their employer as appropriate.

4.304   Can they be used in information services?

Yes. They can be copied, distributed electronically, printed, given away or sold, either freely or by licence.

Copying as a condition of export

4.305   Supposing a library or archive contains material which is still in copyright but is of considerable national interest and it is decided to sell this abroad: can anything be done to copy it before it is taken out of the country?

Sometimes, yes. If the condition of export is that a copy is made to be retained in this country, it is not an infringement to make the copy or to receive it to be kept in a library or archive.

Public administration

4.306   Are there any other reasons for being allowed to copy?

Yes. Another reason is what the Act calls public administration.

4.307   What does 'public administration' cover?

Not as much as it would at first seem! The Act lists four areas:

- Parliamentary proceedings
- judicial proceedings
- Royal Commission
- statutory inquiry.

4.308 **What can be copied?**

There are no limits. The Act says: 'Copyright is not infringed by anything done for the purposes of Parliamentary or judicial proceedings.' The only qualification is a further allowance to the effect that if anything is copied for the proceedings and subsequently published in those proceedings that is not itself an infringement of copyright.

4.309 **Can material be copied to answer a freedom of information request?**

The CDPA does not mention freedom of information (FOI) but the Information Commissioner's Office has ruled that where it is necessary to copy a document to answer an FOI request, that document could be copied without infringing copyright, provided that the copy supplied is clearly marked to say that it was for an FOI request and any further use of that copy would constitute infringement of copyright.

Material open to public inspection

4.310 **Many libraries contain registers of various kinds and often act as a public information point for local authority activity such as planning applications or electoral registers. Can any of this material be copied?**

When material is open to the public as part of a statutory requirement, or is on a statutory register, the material can be copied without infringing the copyright in that material, so long as this is done with the authority of the appropriate person. The purpose of the copying must be to make it available for inspection at a more convenient time or place or to enable the right of inspection to be exercised in some other way to satisfy statutory requirement.

4.311 **Can only single copies to individuals be made?**

Not necessarily. The material may be copied, copies issued to the public, or put on a website without infringing copyright.

4.312 **Are there any limitations on this?**

Yes. The one condition is that the material is not commercially available to the public. If it is, these rules do not apply.

4.313 Is this limited to requests by individual members of the public?

No. Where a document open for public inspection contains information of a general scientific, technical, economic or commercial interest, that information may be copied, published or put on a website provided that this is done with the authority of the appropriate person and the material is not commercially available to the general public.

4.314 Who is an 'appropriate person'?

An appropriate person is the person who is required to make the material open to the public or the person maintaining the register. Such persons can authorise libraries and others to make copies as described above.

4.315 Can a member of the public copy an electoral register?

Yes, and the limits are not set down legally although there may be physical or financial restraints to consider if large quantities are needed. Where whole registers are wanted it would be better for a reader to contact the local registrar.

4.316 Are all forms of the electoral register available to be copied?

No. The full register is available only to a limited number of organisations such as local councils, the police and similar agencies. This is not publicly available and cannot be copied. The publicly available version contains only those names of members of the public who have not asked for their names to be withheld from the public register and this shorter version can be copied.

4.317 Does this also apply to statutory registers such as registers of voters?

Apparently not, because no mention is made of statutory registers in the relevant section of the Act. However, the SI refers specifically to statutory registers in this section, so it is unclear just what is allowed.

4.318 Do these regulations apply only to UK materials?

Mostly, yes. The two exceptions are material made open to the public by the European Patent Office and the World Intellectual Property Organization, both intended to assist the process of patent registration.

4.319 What about material which constitutes public records?

Any material that constitutes public records under the appropriate public records

Acts which are open to public inspection can be copied and copies supplied to anyone, with the authority of the appropriate officer as appointed under the relevant Acts of Parliament.

4.320 **What if an Act of Parliament actually requires that something be copied for the processes of law?**

If the copying is a required part of an Act of Parliament then it is not an infringement of copyright.

4.321 **Supposing a copy is needed because of a national crisis such as war?**

This may be allowed as being in the public interest. The Act allows that nothing shall be done or prevented which the rule of law requires for the national interest.

4.322 **Does the existence of a separate typographical copyright prevent libraries and others from copying materials?**

No. The law specifically states that anything that can be done by way of copying with a copyright work can also be done to the typographical layout of that work.

Disabled persons

4.323 **Supposing someone needs to use a work that is in printed form but they have a disability which prevents them from reading it. Can copies be made for them?**

Fortunately, legislation permits copies to be made for disabled people.

4.324 **Who qualifies as disabled person?**

A disabled person is one who has a physical or mental disability which prevents them enjoying the work which they wish to use to substantially the same degree as a person who does not have that disability. But it does not apply to visually impaired persons whose access to copyright works could be improved by the use of corrective lenses to a level that is normally acceptable without a special level of light.

4.325 **How much may be copied for a disabled person?**

The whole of a work may be copied into a format suitable for a person with disabilities to use.

4.326 What formats can be used?

The law does not specify or limit the formats to be used but it includes any format that enables disabled persons to access the work, including accessing it as feasibly and comfortably as a person who is not a disabled person.

4.327 Are there any restrictions?

Yes, a number of limitations are put on this exception:

- The disabled person must have access to a lawful copy of the work.
- The work must not be commercially available in the format needed.
- The copy must be made by a disabled person or on behalf of a disabled person.
- The copy must be made for the disabled person's personal use.
- The copy made must have sufficient acknowledgement of its source (bibliographic reference would seem to be implied).
- The copy must be marked to show it was made under the legislation relating to making copies for disabled people.

4.328 What does 'lawful copy' mean?

While it is not defined, it would seem to be acceptable that it means that the copy of the work was made under the terms of this Act and was issued to the public lawfully.

4.329 Can a library or other organisation make copies on behalf of a disabled person?

Yes, an authorised body may make and supply a copy and also communicate it, make it available, distribute or lend the item, but there are restrictions:

- The copy must be made for the disabled person's personal use.
- The work must not be commercially available in the format needed.
- The authorised body must have lawful access to the whole or part of the document.
- The document must be a published document.
- If the copy is made by an educational establishment conducted for profit then it must ensure that any accessible copies are used only for educational purposes.

4.330   What is an 'accessible copy'?

An accessible copy is a version of the work which enables a fuller enjoyment of the work by a disabled person. This includes navigation systems to enable the disabled person to find their way round the work but does not include making changes to the work that are not necessary to make it accessible.

4.331   Can a library or other organisation charge for making the copy?

Yes, but no more than the actual cost of making it.

4.332   Can a library or other organisation make a copy for another organisation?

Yes, provided that both organisations are authorised bodies and the purpose is only to make an accessible copy for a disabled person.

4.333   What is an 'authorised body'?

An authorised body is an educational establishment or an organisation not conducted for profit. The authorised body must also observe a complex and strict regime of conditions set out in Statutory Instrument 2018/995.

4.334   Can one disabled person pass the copy on to another?

Yes, provided that the second person fulfils all the criteria set out above. But they must not copy the copy they have and pass that on instead.

4.335   What if several students in a school, college or university all need copies in alternative formats?

The copies can be made provided the institution making the copies has lawful possession of an original copy of the work. The other conditions set out for copying for individuals above also apply. In addition, if the institution making the copy is an educational establishment (see Section 4.181), then the staff must make sure the copies are used only for educational purposes.

4.336   Making these copies can be costly. Can the institution keep an electronic file so as to make copies for other students in the future?

Yes, this is allowed, with some restrictions.

4.337   What are these restrictions?

In addition to the conditions set out for individuals above the institution making the copy must:

- keep records of copies made and to whom they are supplied
- keep records of any intermediate copies lent to other institutions
- allow the copyright owner or their representative (perhaps the CLA) to access these records
- notify the copyright owner or representative of any copies transferred or lent to other organisations.

4.338   Does this mean the copies in alternative formats can be lent?

Yes, but only to another organisation fulfilling all the criteria set out earlier.

4.339   Are there any other rules?

One important rule is that when the original is in electronic form and contains electronic management data about ownership, authorship or other information, any copies made in electronic form must also contain this information and it must not be deleted.

4.340   What about licences?

Where a licensing scheme offers the facility to make copies in alternative formats, this licence must be adhered to.

4.341   What is the advantage of copying under licence rather than just making the copies?

Where multiple copies are needed the use of the licence saves a lot of bureaucratic paperwork and record keeping.

Section 5
Artistic works

Definition

5.1   **What is the definition of an artistic work?**

The definition of artistic works is given in the CDPA as:

- graphic works such as paintings, drawings, diagrams, maps, charts and plans, engravings, lithographs, etchings or woodcuts, sculpture, collage; this includes the surface design of manufactured products such as pottery and textiles
- photographs (including slides and negatives as well as microforms)
- architectural works (including buildings of any kind)
- works of artistic craftsmanship, such as jewellery or pottery.

5.2   **Does the work have to have some artistic quality to be protected by copyright?**

No, but see the notes below on works of artistic craftsmanship where the situation is somewhat different. Otherwise quality is not a requirement but the usual tests of originality and showing some skill and creativity apply.

5.3   **What is the definition of a photograph?**

A photograph is defined as: 'photograph means a recording of light or other radiation on any medium on which an image is produced or from which an image may by any means be produced, and which is not part of a film'.

5.4   **Do microforms qualify for copyright?**

Certainly. A microfilm or microfiche ('microforms' for short) is a photograph and attracts copyright in the same way as a photograph itself. A microfilm containing several different documents may also be a database (see Section 9).

5.5   **What happens if the work which has been microfilmed is still in copyright?**

There are then two copyrights, one in the original document and one in the microform. To make the new copy would require the consent of the original copyright owner.

5.6   **Supposing the work that has been microfilmed is out of copyright?**

There is probably still copyright in the microform as a photograph even though the work photographed is out of copyright. Some authorities argue that there is no copyright in the photograph of a 'flat' object such as a document but others would argue that change of medium (from paper to photograph) requires sufficient skill to create a new original work. But a straightforward photocopy or scanned copy of the work would not attract a new copyright as there would be insufficient skill shown in making the copy to justify a new copyright.

Example: A microform of *Magna Carta* would attract copyright as a photograph but the *Magna Carta* certainly would not.

5.7   **What is the situation if enlargements are made from the microform?**

The enlargements can be an infringement of copyright in the microform and also copyright in the original document, if the original is still in copyright, or of just the microform if that is still in copyright but the document filmed is not.

Authors and their rights

5.8   **Who counts as the author of an artistic work?**

The author of an artistic work is defined in the same terms as for a literary, dramatic or musical work (see Sections 4.13 and following). This includes, in the case of photographs, the photographer.

5.9   **Do authors of artistic works have moral rights?**

Yes. They are described in Sections 3.2–3.7. Note that authors of artistic works have the right to be named as the author if the work is exhibited in public. This right has to be asserted before the exhibition takes place, to be valid.

Ownership of copyright

5.10   Who owns the copyright in an artistic work?

Generally, ownership of the copyright of an artistic work is defined in the same terms as for a literary, dramatic or musical work (see Sections 3.8 and 4.28 and following). But note that the ownership of the copyright in commissioned paintings, photographs or engravings made before 1 August 1989 belongs to the person commissioning the work if they actually paid for it to be done, not just expenses. See also Sections 3.19 and 4.28 for unpublished works bequeathed to libraries.

5.11   Who owns the copyright in a collection of images?

Each image has its own copyright just like the articles in a periodical (see Section 5:4.25). However, there will also be a copyright in a compilation made up of images. It may also be a database (see Section 9), depending on the way the collection is put together.

5.12   If a library or archive makes its own microforms or digital copies, who owns the copyright?

The copyright belongs to the library or archive. However, if the library or archive commissions an outside bureau to make the copies, ownership of the copyright depends on the contract between the two parties. Where the copies have been bought from a commercial company, the copyright remains with that company, despite the status of the original documents filmed.

5.13   Quite often copies of photographs supplied by libraries or archives state that, although they are old, the copyright is owned by the library or archive from which permission must be sought to make copies or publish the photograph. Is this legal?

The position is that the library or archive owns the photographs but not necessarily the copyright in them. They may well impose restrictions on the subsequent use of the photographs, and that is their right as owners of the physical photographs. But they may not own the copyright in these works. If conditions are imposed, such as payment for publication, then once these are met, the library or archive has no further claim on the photograph and certainly not the copyright in it.

Owners' rights

5.14 **What rights does the owner of copyright in artistic works have?**

The owner has the same rights as for literary, dramatic or musical works (see Section 4). Note that the right to exhibit an artistic work is not a right the copyright owner enjoys, despite general belief to the contrary. This is not true for literary, dramatic or musical works. See Section 4.43.

5.15 **Do people who appear in photographs have any rights over them?**

Not under copyright law, but this is an area where particular care needs to be exercised. Although the person taking the photograph (or their employer if appropriate) owns the copyright, the use of that photograph may be restricted by other legal considerations. For example, using the image of a famous person to promote a product or event can lead to claims of loss of revenue because the celebrity would have made a charge for having their name used in this way, even if the copyright in the photograph is owned by the person using it. Even more important can be the use of photographs that depict people in private situations such as in their home, hospital or even receiving medical attention in the street. The situation is public, but the event is private, and people have sued for use of photographs under human rights legislation in these circumstances. Use of general street scenes or groups is probably acceptable. Particular care needs to be exercised with photographs of children and these should not be used without the written consent of the parent or guardian.

5.16 **What about taking photographs?**

A photograph of an artistic work (say a statue or painting) is an infringement of the artist's copyright unless the work is a building, a sculpture or a work of artistic craftsmanship, and is on permanent public display in a public open space or premises open to the public.

5.17 **What counts as 'a work of artistic craftsmanship'?**

The law does not give a definition but the courts have generally (although exceptions can be found) ruled that the work must demonstrate craftsmanship in the making of it and some artistic merit, measured as being appealing to the eye. This is all rather subjective, and different judgements give different slants on these ideas!

5.18   **What constitutes 'open to the public'?**

This is not defined but it would certainly be a street or thoroughfare and any building to which the public had access in the normal course of events. Presumably libraries, museums and art galleries are open to the public, although particular parts of them may not be, so these would not count (e.g. strongrooms, vaults, closed stacks, and so on). Rooms in town halls and other similar buildings are more difficult to define.

5.19   **What constitutes 'permanent'?**

Unfortunately this is not defined. Obviously something on loan for, say, six months, could not be permanent. Something might be on display for six months and then taken away and be counted as permanent because it was intended to be so when it was put on display in the first place.

Copying

5.20   **The owners of some buildings charge copying fees to photograph artistic works housed in them even though the works must surely be out of copyright. Is this allowed?**

This is not a copyright fee but a copying fee. Owners have the right to set out rules for accessing their premises and these may include a prohibition on taking photos. The owners of a cathedral, for example, cannot claim there is copyright in a medieval painting but this does not stop them from charging for the privilege of having access to photograph their property. The painting is their property even though the copyright has long since expired.

5.21   **What about making a photographic image of a painting?**

Photocopying, microfilming or making a transparency, slide or digital image of a drawing, engraving or painting are all infringements.

5.22   **What about making a model of something in a painting?**

It is also an infringement to make a three-dimensional model of a picture, photograph or painting in just the same way as photographing a statue is an infringement.

5.23   **Does this include making a copy using 3D printing?**

Yes. The technique used does not matter: it is the copying that is important.

Whether the model would be protected by copyright is hard to say. If it is an exact model then it could be argued that it is not copyright because, although skill and labour had been used to make it, there was no actual original creativity. Certainly the use of 3D printing would not create a new copyright work as there is no use of skill or technique to create the model.

However, if the model was selective in the detail reproduced (say a small model of a ship) or it had been scaled up or down, then it might be possible to argue that not only craftsmanship but also technical skill had been used, so the model qualified for copyright. Even if the original was out of copyright the model could still qualify.

5.24 Will 3D printing always infringe copyright?

No. Many items that will be copied using 3D will not be protected by copyright. For example, items of furniture such as a chair or do-it-yourself materials such as screws or tools. They are protected by either patent or design right, if protected at all, and making a single copy is not an infringement. Making multiple copies and selling them certainly would be a serious offence, though.

5.25 What happens if a photograph (or television programme) happens to include a piece of copyright material in the background? Say, an interview in front of a recent painting in a gallery?

Incidental copying of this nature is not an infringement – but it would be if the photographer or TV producer deliberately intended the painting or sculpture to be included. However, if the programme were about a particular painter whose works were still in copyright then the inclusion would be deliberate and would infringe the artist's copyright. There might still be a defence of using the image for criticism or review but it would depend on the nature of the programme.

5.26 Supposing the library or archive holds a painting which it wishes to reproduce as a slide, poster or postcard?

If the painting is out of copyright or if the picture is of a statue or something similar on permanent public display, then there is no problem. Remember the slide, poster or postcard will attract copyright, which will be owned by the photographer, the library or archive, depending on whether the photographer was an employee of the library or archive, or the library or archive simply commissioned the taking of the photograph!

5.27   **Supposing there is an exhibition of children's work and the library wants to use this for publicity material or to publish it?**

Technically the copyright belongs to the children individually and the permission of the child or guardian is necessary before works can be reproduced. Some teachers might argue that the copyright belongs to the school but the child is not employed there (at least not in the sense of having gainful employment there!) and the teacher cannot claim the copyright because the child actually did the painting.

Issue of copies to the public

5.28   **Does issuing to the public apply to artistic works?**

Issuing copies to the public is restricted as for literary, dramatic and musical works. See Sections 4.40 and following.

Performing the work

5.29   **Is it an infringement to perform an artistic work?**

There is no performing right, including the right of exhibition, for artistic works.

5.30   **Can the owner of a painting or other artistic work put it on public display?**

Yes. The right of display is not one of the acts restricted by copyright. Once the work has been purchased the owner of the work may display it but this does not alter the rights of the copyright owner to reproduce the work, e.g. on postcards, photographs, slides, and so on. But note that exhibiting an anonymous copyright artistic work which has not been previously published or exhibited has the effect of starting the period of copyright protection all over again to 70 years from first exhibiting the work.

Communicating the work to the public by electronic means

5.31   **Supposing a television programme included a shot of a painting or sculpture. Would this be counted as broadcasting?**

Yes, unless it was incidentally included, as mentioned in Section 5.25.

5.32   Supposing the television programme is a news item about an artist who has just died and that is being reported.

Then, to include one of the artist's paintings as part of the news might not be an infringement because this would be reporting current events (see Section 5.71).

5.33   Does putting a photograph or picture on a website, or making it available through social media networks, require permission from the copyright owner?

Yes, unless it is out of copyright. Putting anything on website is 'communicating the work to the public by electronic means' and is an infringement of the copyright owner's rights.

Adaptation and translation

5.34   Is there a right of adaptation in artistic works? How does it work?

Yes. Most forms of adaptation are really copying. So, to make a model of a painting is really an adaptation of the original to a different form as mentioned in Sections 5.22–23). For example, making a three-dimensional 'touchy-feely' version of a map would infringe, as it is making a three-dimensional work from a two-dimensional one. Where technical devices such as 3D printing are used to make a three-dimensional version of a map this is also an infringement and a new copyright work might have been created, as the format is different. However, it would still be an infringing copy.

Lending and rental

5.35   Are artistic works subject to lending and rental restrictions?

Yes.

5.36   Does this mean that libraries, archives and galleries may not lend artistic works?

Not altogether. In the first place, this restriction applies only to material acquired on or after 1 December 1996. Second, lending (charging no more than operational costs) is allowed for any library except a public library.

5.37   Why are public libraries excluded?

Because the Act specifically states that public libraries, whether or not a charge is made, cannot lend these materials, except those acquired before December 1996, or under licence.

5.38   Will they be covered by the PLR Scheme?

No. This is limited to textual material.

5.39   Supposing there is no licensing scheme available?

The Secretary of State has the power to implement a scheme, subject to appropriate payment, as determined by the Copyright Tribunal if necessary.

Crown and Parliamentary copyright

5.40   Are artistic works subject to Crown and Parliamentary copyright?

Yes, just like literary, dramatic and musical works, but note the duration of copyright is different.

Publication right

5.41   Does publication right apply to artistic works?

Yes, see Sections 4.93 and following.

Typographical copyright

5.42   Does typographical copyright apply to artistic works?

It depends on the nature of the work. It would be hard to argue there was typographical arrangement in a photograph or plate of an artistic work but there would be typographical arrangement in a map, for example. So it would apply in that case.

Duration of copyright

5.43   How long does copyright in artistic works last?

Although artistic works are protected in the same way as literary, dramatic or musical works, there are some important differences. Some of the rules are repeated here for ease of reference. The rules about extended and revived copyright described in Sections 3.8 and 3.25–26 also apply to artistic works.

5.44   Do the rules about works originating in the EEA (see Section 4.101 and following) also apply?

Yes the rules in this area are the same. To save unnecessary repetition the term '70 years' has been used in the following paragraphs but marked * to remind you that the EEA and non-EEA rules apply.

5.45   Are there differences for published and unpublished works?

Yes. Most published artistic works are protected for 70* years from the end of the year in which the author died, but if the author died before 1 January 1969 and the work was published posthumously then copyright expires 50 years after publication. It is important to examine each type of work, especially photographs, separately. The duration of different types of published and unpublished artistic works is set out in the following paragraphs.

Published works – generally

5.46   Artistic works with an author – published – generally

See specific formats listed below. Otherwise usually copyright expires 70* years from the end of the year in which the author died. This includes surface design of manufactured products such as pottery or textiles, although this regulation will not come into force until 2020. Until then surface design is protected for 25 years from first being used.

5.47   Anonymous and pseudonymous artistic works – published

Essentially copyright in these works lasts 70* years from the end of the year in which they were created, but if they were first made available to the public during that period, then it lasts 70* years from the end of the year in which that took place.

5.48   Anonymous and pseudonymous artistic works – unpublished

Essentially copyright in these works lasts for 70* years from the end of the year in which they were created or from being first made available to the public. However, where a work was created before 1 January 1969 copyright protection must last until 31 December 2039 regardless of the assumed date of creation. Note that the government carried out a consultation into simplifying these rules but decided against making any changes in 2015.

5.49 Is 'first made available to the public' the same as 'published'?

No. In the case of artistic works it includes:

- exhibitions
- included in a broadcast or cable television programme
- included in a film.

Engravings

5.50 Engravings – published – author known

If published after the artist's death and before 1 January 1969: protected until year of publication + 50 years. Otherwise protected until year of artist's death + 70* years.

5.51 Engravings – unpublished – author known

If unpublished and the artist died before 1 January 1969: protected until 31 December 2039. Otherwise protected from year of artist's death + 70* years.

5.52 Engravings – published – author unknown

Copyright expires 70* years after publication.

5.53 Engravings – unpublished – author unknown

Copyright in unpublished anonymous engravings created but not published or made available to the public before 1 January 1969 expires on 31 December 2039. If the engraving was made after 1 January 1969 then copyright expires 70* years from creation. Note that the government carried out a consultation into simplifying these rules but decided against making any changes in 2015.

See also 'Crown and Parliamentary copyright', Section 5.61.

Photographs

5.54 Photographs – published – author known

For photographs taken before 1 June 1957 copyright expires 70* years after the author died. If the photograph was published before 1 August 1989 and the author had died before 1 January 1969 then copyright expires 50 years after the date of publication. If the author died before 1 January 1969 and the photo was published then copyright expires 70* years after the death of the author.

5.55   Photographs – published – author unknown

If the photo was created before 1 June 1957 copyright expires 70* years after creation or 70* years after first being made available to the public if this occurs within the 70-year period. If the photograph was published before 1 August 1989 then copyright expires 70* years after publication.

5.56   Photographs – unpublished – author known

If the photograph was taken before 1 June 1957 then copyright expires 70* years after the death of the author.

If the author died before 1 January 1969 the copyright expires 31 December 2039. If the author died after 1 January 1969 then copyright expires 70* years after the death of the author.

5.57   Photographs – unpublished – author unknown

If the photograph was taken before 1 June 1957 then copyright expires 70* years after it was taken or, if made available to the public in that period, 70* years from when that took place. If the photo was taken after that date and has not been made available to the public then copyright expires 31 December 2039.

If the work was first made available to the public after 1 January 1969 then copyright expires 70* years from when that took place.

5.58   How long is the microform or digital image protected?

If the author can be established, then for 70* years from the year of the author's death; otherwise 70* years from the year in which the image was made available to the public.

5.59   Unpublished works generally

Works of which the creator died before 1 January 1969, and were unpublished at the time of death, are protected until 31 December 2039. All other works are protected for 70* years from the end of the year in which the author died. Note that the government carried out a consultation into simplifying these rules but decided against making any changes in 2015.

Typographical arrangement

5.60   What about typographical arrangement?

If typographical arrangement does exist in an artistic work, maps for example, then it will expire 25 years after first publication. But note that a digital map may also be considered a database if individual items on the map can be individually accessed.

Crown and Parliamentary copyright

5.61   What about the duration of Crown and Parliamentary copyright?

Where copyright in an artistic work (other than an engraving or photograph) is owned by the Crown and the work was made before 1 August 1989, copyright expires 50 years from the end of the year in which the work was created. This is very useful for maps, as Ordnance Survey (OS) paper maps created more than 50 years ago are out of copyright. The privatisation of Ordnance Survey in 2015 does not affect the status of maps created by OS before that date. Works made after this date are subject to the same rules as literary works (see Sections 4.119 and following). Copyright in published engravings made before 1 August 1989 expires 50 years from the year of publication. Copyright in an unpublished engraving made before 1 August 1989 expires on 31 December 2039. However, copyright in unpublished photographs taken on or after 1 August 1989 will last for 125 years subject to their not being published commercially within the first 75 years; those taken on or after 1 June 1957 but before 1 August 1989 would have protection until the end of 2039; and those taken before 1 June 1957 had protection for 50 years from the end of the year in which they were taken and are therefore now out of copyright.

Copyright in works that are owned by either or both Houses of Parliament expires at the end of 50 years from the year in which the work was created.

Exceptions

5.62   Are artistic works subject to the same exceptions as literary works?

Yes, but there are some differences.

Private copying

5.63   Is private copying for personal use allowed for artistic works?

No. The only copying for personal use is under fair dealing.

Fair dealing

5.64   Are artistic works subject to fair dealing?

Artistic works are subject to fair dealing in a similar way to literary, dramatic and musical works but there are some differences.

5.65   What constitutes 'fair dealing' in an artistic work?

This is undefined, as for other works. However, the same general rules apply (see Sections 4.132 and following).

5.66   Do the reasons for fair dealing – non-commercial research or private study, criticism or review and reporting current events – still apply to artistic works?

Yes. The reasons are just the same. Except that the rules are different for reporting current events.

Research for a non-commercial purpose

5.67   How can something be copied fairly when it is an artistic work? Surely the whole of the work would be copied?

Perhaps. Fair dealing does not exclude copying all of the work.

Example: An art student needs to study the different ways of portraying Hercules. The student could take photographs of modern statues, paintings and drawings for personal use to carry out the research. The photographs must not be sold or published or they would not constitute fair dealing for the purposes of non-commercial research. This limitation would not apply if work was a statue on permanent public display. If copies of Hercules that met the student's needs were available commercially then this copying could be considered unfair.

5.68   What about people who go to art galleries (and libraries) and make paintings of other people's paintings?

This would be considered as fair because those people's paintings are for private study. The copy would have sufficient original input from the copying painter to qualify for copyright protection in its own right but might still be challenged as an infringement of the copyright in the original work if that was still in copyright.

5.69 **Can a student include a copy of an artistic work, say a photograph of a statue, in a thesis?**

Yes. This is for research and also providing the answer to an examination, so it is covered by educational copying (see Section 4.177), which still requires the copying to be fair. But if the thesis is published then the copyright in the artistic work is infringed.

Private study

5.70 **Are the rules for private study and artistic works the same as for literary works?**

Yes, the rules are same. See Sections 4.144 and following.

Reporting current events

5.71 **Can artistic works be used to report current events?**

For general conditions see Sections 4.164 and following, but the one exception is that photographs may not be used for this purpose. Note that there are no restrictions on reporting for commercial use.

Criticism, review and quotation

5.72 **Can artistic works be used in criticism, review or quotation?**

Artistic works may be reproduced for these purposes provided that there is sufficient acknowledgement of their authorship. There are additional limitations on use for quotations.

5.73 **What constitutes sufficient acknowledgement?**

This is not defined but would presumably include the name of the author at least.

5.74 **Can an artistic work be reproduced in a journal article?**

Only if the purpose is criticism, review or quotation. Simply to include a photograph of a copyright painting to illustrate a point about modern art would not be sufficient justification.

5.75   **Supposing someone wants to include a painting, drawing or map in an article? Is this allowed?**

It is permitted to include as much of the work as is justified by the purpose for which it is being included. For example, if an article on painting techniques included reproduction of a painting, it would not be justified to reproduce the whole painting if copying just part of it would make the point being discussed.

5.76   **What about using a painting or photograph of a piece of sculpture to advertise an exhibition?**

This would not be allowed.

Text and data mining

5.77   **Is it allowed to copy an artistic work for analysing data?**

Yes. A work may be copied for the purposes of computational analysis of the contents. For example, data contained in a map might be needed.

5.78   **Are there any restrictions?**

Yes. See Sections 4.153 and following for details.

5.79   **What about sale catalogues which include photographs of copyright materials?**

That is allowed. There is a specific clause allowing the copying of works to advertise them for sale.

Educational copying

See also Sections 4.170 and following for literary, dramatic and musical works.

5.80   **Can artistic works be copied for educational purposes?**

Artistic works may be copied by either teachers or students for the purposes of illustrating instruction. The copying must be fair.

5.81   **What about examination questions?**

It is permitted to copy examination questions, for setting questions or answering them. But the use must be within the limits of what is considered fair dealing.

5.82   What about educational licensing schemes?

These apply to artistic works in various ways. See Section 10.

5.83   What is to be done for the classroom teacher who wants multiple copies of, say, a photograph, for classroom use?

This is not permitted. However, each student might claim fair dealing to make their own copy for non-commercial research purposes. The rules for multiple copying for educational use are described in Sections 4.183 and following but note that artistic works are excluded unless they are embedded in the text to be copied. Also any licensing restrictions must be adhered to.

5.84   Can artistic works be made available through electronic terminals in the same way as other works?

Yes. See Section 4.186 for more details.

5.85   Can a slide be included in, say, a film or video?

Perhaps. This may be permitted for the purposes of illustration during teaching. Otherwise it will probably infringe.

5.86   Can slides or photographs be made of artistic works for classroom use or teaching?

Yes. See the educational copying paragraphs in Section 4 for more details.

5.87   Can copies be made of maps for classroom use?

A single copy can be made by the person giving or receiving instruction but photocopies for classroom use cannot be made except under the licence of the copyright owner. In the case of OS maps which are less than 50 years old, OS provides a licensing scheme for education. See Section 10.

Library and archive copying

See also Section 4.

5.88   Can libraries and archives copy artistic works in their collections in the same way as textual materials?

Yes. Remember the term 'library' includes archives, museums and galleries, which are included in the term 'qualifying libraries'. See Sections 4.195 and following for the definition.

5.89 **What is to be done for a reader who wants a copy of a photograph?**

This is a bit tricky. Libraries can copy a reasonable proportion of a work that is not a periodical, but whether copying the whole of a photograph could count as a reasonable proportion is open to debate.

5.90 **What about copying maps for users?**

Again, a reasonable proportion of the map may be copied. But see Section 10 relating to OS.

5.91 **What about licences issued by publishers?**

These are really a contract between the library and the copyright owner, who is allowing the library to do certain things the law does not. As owner of the copyright the publisher is entitled to do anything it wishes with its property! Failure to observe the conditions of such a licence is a breach of contract as well as an infringement of copyright. But note that the licence cannot overrule the exception to allow copying of a reasonable proportion. See also Section 10.

5.92 **Supposing an article in a periodical is accompanied by a photograph?**

This can safely be copied, as the Act makes it clear that accompanying materials can legitimately be copied, whether or not they are artistic works as such. But the photograph cannot be copied by itself – only as part of the article.

5.93 **What about copying artistic works that have not been published?**

The conditions are the same as for literary works. See Section 4 for details.

5.94 **Are there any restrictions on copying artistic works for readers?**

Yes. The same rules apply as for literary works. See Section 4 for details about purposes and declarations to be made by the reader.

5.95   **Can the library or archive create an electronic version and make it available to the public?**

Yes, provided the conditions set out in Section 4 are observed, plus any licensing conditions that apply to the purchase of or access to the material.

5.96   **Are libraries allowed to supply copies of artistic works through interlibrary copying?**

Yes, in the same way as for literary works. See Section 4.

5.97   **What if a library or archive has lost its copy of an artistic work? Can a replacement be obtained from another library or archive?**

Yes. Copying for replacement or preservation is allowed. See Section 4 for details.

5.98   **Can artistic works be copied as a condition of export?**

Like literary works, an article of cultural or historical importance may be copied if a condition of the export is that a copy be made and deposited in an appropriate library or archive.

5.99   **What about material open for public inspection?**

No specific mention is made of artistic works, with regard to material open to public inspection.

5.100   **Can artistic works be copied for public administration purposes?**

Yes, allowances apply to artistic works in the same way as to literary works.

Droit de suite or resale right
5.101   **Does droit de suite exist in the UK?**

Yes. For details see Section 12.11

Disabled persons
5.102   **Do the rules for disabled people apply to artistic works?**

Yes, just like literary, dramatic and musical works. See Sections 4.323 and following.

Section 6

Sound recordings and performers' rights

Definition

6.1   **What is the definition of a sound recording?**

The definition of a sound recording is not limited in any way by format. It is any form of recording of sounds from which sounds may be reproduced. So it includes wax cylinders, vinyl discs, audio cassettes, compact discs and DVDs. It also includes sounds recorded and stored in digital form from which sounds can be reproduced.

6.2   **Do the sounds have to be human voices or produced by musical instruments?**

No. The sounds could be of birdsong or a steam train, for example.

Authorship

Remember that this section applies to the recording and not to the content. Any music or words recorded will be protected as literary or musical works (see Sections 4 and 6.7)

6.3   **Who is the author of a sound recording?**

The producer. Remember this is only the physical record, content of the recording is a separate matter.

6.4   **Who counts as the producer?**

This term is defined as the 'person by whom the arrangements necessary for the making of the sound recording are made'.

6.5   **Does the producer of a sound recording enjoy moral rights?**

No.

Ownership

6.6 Who owns the copyright in a sound recording?

It is owned by the recording company that produced the physical carrier of the recording if it is a commercial recording. If it is produced privately by an individual, then the individual owns the copyright. See also Section 3.19 for unpublished materials bequeathed to archives and libraries. If the recording is subject to extended or revived copyright (see Section 6.31) then special rules apply.

6.7 Who owns the content of a sound recording?

It is very important to distinguish between the copyright in the sound recording and the copyright in the material recorded.

Examples: A recording of a song by the Beatles has all sorts of copyrights – the song, the music, the arrangement and the performance. In addition, there is a copyright in the actual sound recording, which is quite separate. Similarly, an interview for an oral history project has a copyright in what the person said, which belongs to the person interviewed. There is also a copyright in the recording made of that interview, which is owned by the person who made the arrangements for making the recording. Again, a recording of Beethoven's Fifth Symphony has a copyright in the recording although there is no longer any copyright in the music itself.

6.8 Who owns the copyright in an interview?

This is important for oral history and similar archives. The speaker owns the copyright in what is said but there is no copyright in the material until it has been recorded. Once it has been recorded the speaker owns the copyright in what has been said, but the person making the recording owns the copyright in the sound recording as such. If the interview is transcribed then the person making the transcription may also be entitled to copyright in their transcription.

6.9 Is it necessary to get permission to make such recordings for archives?

It is advisable to obtain the permission of the speaker when the recording is made. Such permission should stipulate for what purposes the recording will be used, especially if it may be used later by a radio programme or television station. See the Oral History Society website for more information. Go to www.ohs.org.uk/advice/ethical-and-legal (consulted 30 July 2018).

Owners' rights

6.10   What rights does the copyright owner have?

Essentially the owner has the same rights as for literary, dramatic, musical or artistic works. See Sections 4.28 and following.

Copying the work

6.11   Does copying include copying from one medium to another?

Yes. To make a copy of a DVD onto a tape is, of course, copying the work. Copying a CD to go onto an iPod actually makes two copies – one on your hard disc and one onto the iPod, both of which are technically infringing copies.

6.12   Supposing the medium on which the work is stored is obsolete? Can copies be made onto a usable type of equipment?

It is not permitted for individuals to do this, although it is possible for libraries and archives to transfer material from one medium to another for preservation purposes.

Issuing copies to the public

6.13   Who has the right to issue copies to the public?

This is an exclusive right of the copyright owner.

Performing the work

6.14   Who has the right to authorise the playing of the work in public?

The copyright owner has the exclusive right to authorise the playing of the recording. Note that licences for playing sound recordings and the contents of them are available. See Section 10.

6.15   Does this mean that if a library has a collection of sound recordings it is not allowed to put on a public performance of them?

This can be done either with non-copyright material (because it is too old to be protected), or with material in which the library holds the copyright, or if the library is covered by a performing rights licence and a Phonographic Performance Ltd (PPL) licence. See Section 10.

6.16   Supposing the library holds oral history recordings. Can these be played publicly?

Only if the library owns the copyright in both the words spoken and the sound recording itself, or if those taking part in the interview have given their permission.

6.17   How can the library obtain the copyright in the actual words spoken?

This is best done by way of an agreement with the interviewee at the time of the interview. Failure to do this could lead to infringement of the speaker's copyright. See Section 6.9 for where to find detailed guidance on this.

6.18   What about children's events in libraries where they sing along?

It depends on the type of event. Briefly, events where there is live singing but no instruments or recorded music do not need a licence; events including live music with instruments or recorded music do need a licence.

6.19   If the library has a collection of sound recordings, can they be played on the library's premises?

They can be played for private listening in carrels or somewhere similar, provided that not more than one person has access to the same recording at the same time, otherwise this could be considered a public performance. Otherwise they can be played only if the library (or the library authority) has PRS for Music and PPL licences which cover that building, including areas used only by the staff, such as staff rooms and eating areas. Note that PRS for Music and PPL now issue joint licences to make it easier to cover both live and recorded music (see Section 10.30 for details). Outside these limitations, public playing of copyright material is an infringement. Check with the authority that owns the library premises to see if the library is covered by such a licence. This also applies to films, videos, television broadcasts and radio.

6.20   What about material available on the internet in libraries?

It seems likely that you need a PRS licence to do this unless it is made available through single-access terminals.

Communicating the work to the public by electronic means

6.21   Who has the right to communicate the work to the public by electronic means?

This is an exclusive right of the copyright owner unless the work or a copy of the work has been lawfully acquired by the library and is made available to the public through dedicated terminals. See Section 4 for more details.

6.22   Presumably libraries do not have to worry about restrictions on broadcasting?

Not true. There is an increasing interest in local studies and live comments from the past, as well as folk music and recent broadcast interviews. Where this material has been prepared, recorded or given to the library or archive, it may well be in demand from local or national broadcasting stations. To allow this to be used in this way is an infringement unless the original owner gave express permission when the recording was made.

Adaptation

6.23   Who has the right of adaptation?

Adaptation from one format to another may be allowed for preservation purposes but any attempt to adapt the actual content of the recording (re-working a modern pop song to a jazz format, for example) needs permission from the copyright owner of the music.

Lending and rental

6.24   If this right is an exclusive right of the owner, does this mean that lending services for audio materials are not allowed?

Basically, yes. Sound recordings may not be rented to the public without the copyright owner's permission. They can be lent by qualifying libraries (see Sections 4.195 and following) provided the fee charged only covers the cost of administration, but they cannot be lent by public libraries without a licence of some kind. See Section 10.

6.25   Supposing a work is held by a library in printed form, as an audio cassette or as an e-book. What is the position then?

All these formats are now covered by the PLR Scheme.

6.26   Does this mean that libraries cannot lend records?

Not altogether. First, this restriction applies only to material acquired on or after 1 August 1989. Second, there are special agreements with the production industries to allow lending facilities under specified terms. It is best to check the conditions of purchase of particular materials in the library or any licensing arrangements. (See also Section 10.)

6.27   Why are public libraries excluded?

Because the Copyright Act stipulates that lending by public libraries of these materials is an infringement. Furthermore the regulations on lending prohibit public libraries from lending material not covered by the PLR Scheme.

6.28   Supposing there is no licensing scheme available?

The Secretary of State has the power to implement a scheme, subject to appropriate payment, as determined by the Copyright Tribunal if necessary.

6.29   What about the rights that performers such as singers or instrumentalists have in sound recordings?

If it is allowed to lend the sound recording then no rights of performers are infringed by that act of lending.

Publication right

6.30   Does publication right apply to sound recordings?

No.

Duration of copyright

6.31   How long does copyright in a sound recording last?

Essentially 70 years from the end of the year in which it was made but if it was released during that period or played in public or communicated to the public, then the 70-year period starts all over again. If the recording was made between 1957 and 1989 and not published in that period then copyright lasts until 31 December 2039. Note that the government carried out a consultation into simplifying these rules but decided against making any changes in 2015. Remember this applies to the actual physical sound recording: the content of the recording, including performances, will be protected separately.

6.32   Are Crown and Parliamentary sound recordings subject to copyright?

These are subject to the usual rules as set out in Sections 6.10–6.31, except that if the recording was made between 1 June 1957 and 1 August 1989 and subsequently published the copyright expires 50 years after publication.

6.33   Do sound recordings have extended and revived copyright?

Yes. There is extended copyright for sound recordings but revived copyright only for literary or musical works which form part of a work of co-authorship (see Section 4.118 for the definition of co-authorship).

Exceptions

Copying for private use

6.34   Is copying for private use allowed for sound recordings?

No. Copying for private use is allowed only under fair dealing (see below).

6.35   Does this mean an individual cannot transfer a sound recording from one medium to another?

Yes. Individuals cannot transfer a recording from, say, vinyl to CD or iPod, or a CD to their PC. Some downloads for music do permit this but it is important to study the conditions when these items are bought.

Fair dealing

6.36   Is there fair dealing in sound recordings?

Yes. See Section 4 for more detailed information on fair dealing generally.

6.37   Is copying for research for a non-commercial purpose allowed?

The same conditions as set out in Section 4 apply.

6.38   Is copying for private study allowed?

Copying for private study is permitted.

Text and data mining

6.39   If a sound recording contains data or information which is needed for computational analysis, can this be copied?

Yes, the same rules apply as for literary works. See Section 4 for details.

Reporting current events

6.40   Can sound recordings be used for reporting current events?

Yes. Short extracts from appropriate recordings can be used for news items and there is no need to acknowledge their source nor is the use restricted to non-commercial use.

Criticism, review and quotation

6.41   Can sound recordings be used for criticism, review or quotation?

Yes, so long as the source is acknowledged. So a broadcast that includes short extracts from sound recordings to provide comment on the work of a singer or composer is allowed.

Library copying

6.42   Can libraries copy sound recordings?

Yes. Basically the same rules apply as in Section 4.

6.43   Can libraries copy sound recordings for preservation purposes?

Yes, again see Section 4 for the rules governing this.

6.44   What can be done if a record or tape is deteriorating rapidly and will be lost if it is not copied?

This can be done in order to replace or preserve the original item. See Section 4 for the conditions attached to doing this.

6.45 **What happens if someone wishes to record a folksong for an archive?**

There are special rules for this. In the first place the song must be of unknown authorship and be unpublished. In other words, it must be a real original folksong. If this really is the case then a recording can be made, so long as the performer does not prohibit this.

6.46 **Can the recording be kept in any local history or academic archive?**

Yes. The archive must be accessible to the public and not conducted for profit or owned by an organisation conducted for profit.

6.47 **Can copies be made from these recordings?**

Yes, provided that the archivist is satisfied that they are for research for a non-commercial purpose or private study only and not more than one copy is supplied to any one person. The usual rules (see Section 4) about providing a written declaration apply.

6.48 **Is there a requirement that they must be paid for?**

No, but if payment is required the cost must take into account the cost attributable to the making of the copy.

6.49 **Can libraries make sound recordings available through dedicated terminals?**

Yes. See Section 4.187.

6.50 **Can they make copies for other archives?**

Yes. The usual rules for interlibrary supply apply as discussed in Section 4.

Educational use

6.51 **Is copying for educational purposes allowed?**

Yes. Essentially the copying must be fair dealing, for illustration only and for a non-commercial purpose. The copying must be done by the person giving or receiving instruction and the source must be acknowledged. The conditions for copying and transmitting to students are described in Section 4.

6.52   What about using sound recordings in the classroom?

If a sound recording is played in the classroom entirely for the purposes of instruction and only students and staff are present, this is not considered a public performance and is allowed. However, if the playing is for entertainment (such as end-of-term relaxation, some kind of club or just during a wet playtime), then this is not allowed except under licence.

6.53   What about multiple copies for classroom use?

Yes, the same rules apply as in Section 4, but note that broadcasts are excluded, so presumably recordings of broadcasts are also excluded.

6.54   What about making sound recordings available electronically through dedicated terminals?

This is permitted as for literary works. See Section 4.187.

6.55   Can sound recordings be copied into different formats for use by disabled people?

Yes. Essentially the same rules apply as for literary, dramatic and musical works. See Sections 4.324 and following for detailed information.

Other restrictions

Copying as a condition of export

6.56   Do the special arrangements for copying materials of historic or cultural importance before export apply to sound recordings?

Yes. If the condition of export is that a copy is made and deposited in a library or archive, then this is not an infringement and the library or archive can make the copy, or receive the copy made elsewhere.

Material open to public inspection

6.57   Do the special conditions about copying such material apply to sound recordings?

Yes. See Sections 4.310 and following for the regulations.

Public administration

6.58 **Can sound recordings be copied for judicial proceedings, Parliamentary proceedings and statutory inquiries, as in the case of literary works?**

Yes. There is no restriction in these cases.

Rights in performances

6.59 **What are rights in performances?**

Anyone who performs a work in any of the defined categories enjoys the right to give consent to the using or copying of that performance.

6.60 **What are the categories of work which attract rights in performances?**

They are listed as:

- dramatic performance, including dance or mime
- musical performance
- reading or recitation of a literary work
- a variety act.

6.61 **If someone recites a poem or makes a speech in an extempore fashion, without any written text or notes, is this a performance?**

No, and they do not enjoy any rights in it unless someone recorded it, in which case it becomes a literary work because it has been recorded (see Section 2.8). They do not enjoy any rights otherwise because the recitation or reading must be of a literary work which, by definition, must already exist.

6.62 **What if the work performed is out of copyright?**

That makes no difference. A performance of Shakespeare's plays attracts rights for those who perform it because they are performing a literary work and it is their performance which is protected – not Shakespeare's copyright.

6.63 **What rights do performers have?**

Essentially the same as copyright owners giving their consent to:

- copying a recording of their performance

- issuing copies of the recording to the public
- lending or renting out recordings of the performance
- making the performance available to the public by electronic means.

6.64   How long do these rights last?

They last for 70 years from the end of the year in which the performance took place, or, if a sound recording of that performance is released during that period, then 70 years from the release of that recording.

6.65   Are performers' rights subject to fair dealing?

Yes, in the same way as other works. This includes copying for non-commercial research, private study, text and data mining, as well as criticism, quotation or review and reporting current events. They can also be copied for illustration for instruction as for sound recordings (see Sections 6.51–2).

Section 7
Films and videos

Definition

7.1 **What is the definition of a film?**

The definition of a film includes anything from which a moving image can by any means be produced. This covers film of all kinds, video, DVD and any other new technologies which produce moving images. Presumably it would also cover devices such as 'What the butler saw' too! Despite its name, a microfilm is not a film but a photograph.

Note that until July 1957 (when the 1956 Act came into force) films were protected only as a series of photographs.

Authorship

7.2 **Who is the author of a film?**

The producer and the principal director. It is presumed that all films have both producers and principal directors and therefore all films are treated as having joint authorship, unless these two functions are performed by the same person. This applies only to films made on or after 1 July 1994. Before that date the author is defined simply as 'the person responsible for making the arrangements necessary for making the film'.

7.3 **Do the authors of films enjoy moral rights?**

Yes, the producer and principal director both enjoy moral rights in the same way as authors of literary works. See Section 3.

Ownership of copyright

7.4 Who owns the copyright in a film?

See Section 3 on ownership for more detailed information. Ownership of many rights in a film depend on the contracts between the various people who made the film. Remember that the film has many copyright elements.

Example: A filmed interview with a songwriter contains several performances of the songwriter's songs and an extract of a film containing performance of some of these songs. The song-writer may own the copyright in his or her words in the interview and the words and music of the songs; the person making the TV programme owns the copyright in the programme as a whole and the film maker owns some elements at least of the copyright in the extract of the film included in the programme.

However, if the film is made by a private person then that person owns the copyright in the film. See also Section 3.19 for unpublished materials bequeathed to archives and libraries.

7.5 Are the rules for extended and revived copyright the same (see Sections 3.25–26)?

Not quite. The extended copyright is owned by the person who owned the copyright on 31 December 1995 but the revived copyright in the film is owned by the principal director or his or her personal representative. But they will not own any revived copyright in the various elements of the film, such as the screenplay and music, and will need to negotiate with the owners of the copyright of these elements, if they are still in copyright, for rights to exploit the revived copyright in the film as a whole.

Owners' rights

7.6 What rights do copyright owners have?

They have the same rights for films and videos as for literary, dramatic and musical works, as detailed below.

Copying films

7.7 Does this include copying from one medium to another?

Yes. To make a copy of, say, a film to a DVD is copying the work.

7.8 **Supposing the medium on which the work is stored is obsolete? Can copies be made onto a usable type of equipment?**

This is now permitted for preservation purposes in libraries and archives. See Section 4 for private copying.

Issuing copies to the public

7.9 **Is issuing copies to the public also an exclusive right of the copyright owner?**

Yes, this is an exclusive right of the owner.

Performing the work

7.10 **What does performing the work actually mean?**

Essentially showing, projecting or allowing the public to view the film in any way.

The owner has the exclusive right to show the work in public. For other matters relating to performance of a work, see Sections 4.44 and following and 6.15 and following, since the same basic rules apply and the same problems arise.

Communicating the work to the public by electronic means

7.11 **What exactly does this mean in practical terms?**

See Section 4.52 and following for details.

Adaptation

7.12 **What would constitute adaptation?**

The owner has the exclusive right to adapt the work, which would include changing the medium in which it was stored or shown, other than outlined above. It would also include taking the story and recreating it as a book or stage play, as this would infringe copyright in the screenplay.

Lending and rental

7.13 **If this right is an exclusive right of the owner, does this mean that lending services for video and DVD materials are not allowed?**

No. Lending by qualifying libraries (other than public libraries) is allowed provided that any charges made cover no more than the administrative costs of making the loan.

7.14   Does this mean that public libraries may no longer lend videos?

Not altogether. In the first place, this restriction applies only to material acquired on or after 1 August 1989. Second, there may well be special agreements with the production industries to allow rental or lending facilities under agreed terms. It is best to check either the conditions of purchase of particular materials in the library or seek advice on the latest situation from CILIP (see 'Useful sources of information').

7.15   Why are public libraries excluded?

Because public libraries may lend only materials which:

- were purchased before December 1996
- are covered by the PLR Scheme
- are covered by special agreements with the industry at large or with specific production companies or their agents.

7.16   Supposing there is no lending scheme available?

The Secretary of State has the power to implement a scheme, subject to appropriate payment, as determined by the Copyright Tribunal if necessary.

7.17   What about shops that rent out DVDs and videos?

They do this by paying the distributor a licence fee and therefore with their agreement.

7.18   What about the rights that performers such as singers or instrumentalists have in films or videos?

If the making of a copy or the lending of the physical carrier of the work is allowed then no rights of performers are infringed by that act of lending.

Duration of copyright

7.19   Do the rules about works originating in the EEA (see Section 4.101 and following) also apply?

Yes, the rules in this area are the same. To save repetition, the 70-year rule is marked

SECTION 7 FILMS AND VIDEOS

with a * to remind you that the EEA or non-EEA rules apply.

7.20 How long does the copyright in a film last?

If the film was made before 1 July 1957 there is no copyright in the film as such. It is treated as a series of photographs (see Section 5) and as a dramatic work (see Section 4). The rules for those two elements apply. Films made after that date are treated differently. Copyright in a film lasts for 70* years from the end of the year in which the last of the following died:

- the principal director
- the author of the screenplay
- the author of the dialogue
- the composer of music specially created for and used in the film.

Registered and unregistered films
7.21 What is a registered film?

From 1924 to 1980 the Board of Trade operated a scheme whereby cinemas had to show a quota of British films. Therefore all films shown in cinemas had to be registered. The duration of copyright in these is complex; if a library holds copies of such films, staff should consult specialist publications (see 'Useful sources of information'). Mostly the duration of copyright in these films is as shown above.

7.22 It is not always easy to find out who all these people are or when they died. What can be done then?

When the identity of at least one of them is known, then copyright expires, as discussed in Sections 4.17 and following.

7.23 What if the identity of none of them can be found?

Then copyright expires 70* years from the end of the year in which the film was made, unless it was made available to the public during that time.

7.24 What happens if it was made available to the public?

Then copyright runs for 70* years from the end of the year in which that took place.

7.25   **Is 'made available to the public' the same as 'published'?**

Not quite. In the context of a film it means being shown in public or included in a broadcast or communicated to the public by electronic means.

7.26   **Sometimes there is nobody particular responsible for making a film. What happens about copyright then?**

If it is not possible say that anyone took on the distinctive responsibilities in Section 7.20 then none of these rules applies and copyright expires 70* years from the end of the year in which the film was made.

7.27   **Does the soundtrack of a film count as a sound recording or a film?**

The soundtrack of a film counts as part of the film and therefore gets the length of protection of the film, but it can also have rights in it as a sound recording in its own right.

Exceptions
Copying for private use

7.28   **Can individuals copy films and videos for their own private use?**

Only within the limits of fair dealing.

7.29   **Does this mean an individual cannot format-shift a film or video?**

Yes. An individual cannot transfer something from, say, 8mm film to DVD or VHS to DVD.

Fair dealing

7.30   **Is there fair dealing in films?**

Yes. See Section 4 for details.

7.31   **Is there fair dealing in research for non-commercial purposes or private study?**

Fair dealing for these purposes applies as for other materials.

7.32   **Is there fair dealing when reporting current events?**

This applies to films, DVDs and so on. See Sections 4.155 and following.

7.33   Is there fair dealing in criticism, review and quotation?

This applies to films, DVDs and so on. See Sections 4.165 and following.

Other restrictions

Text and data mining

7.34   Do the special rules about copying material for text and data mining apply to films?

Yes. In the same way as other materials. See Sections 4.153–15 for details.

Library and archive copying

7.35   Can libraries or archives copy films or videos in their collections?

The same rules apply as for other works. See Section 4.

7.36   Can libraries or archives make copies for other libraries?

Yes. The same rules for interlibrary copying apply as for other materials. See Section 4.

Educational use

7.37   Is it allowed to show films and DVDs in libraries?

It is allowed only if they are viewed by one person at a time through dedicated terminals where others cannot watch at the same time. Showing them to groups, even for educational or children's use, requires a licence either from the Motion Picture Licensing Corporation (MPLC) or Filmbank. See Section 6 on sound recordings for more details.

7.38   What about showing them in the classroom?

This is allowed provided that only the students and teacher view them and it is for the purpose of instruction.

7.39   Can films be copied for classroom use?

Yes. But the same restrictions apply as set out in Section 4. There is an exception for training in the making of films or film soundtracks and then only by the teacher or student themselves and also for a non-commercial purpose.

7.40   Can films and DVDs be made available through dedicated terminals like other works?

Yes, provided all the conditions described in Section 4.187 are complied with. This applies to both educational use and library users.

7.41   What about using films in the classroom?

If a film or video is shown in the classroom of an educational establishment entirely for the purposes of instruction and only students and staff are present, this is not considered a public performance and is allowed. Use for recreational purposes (see Section 6.52) is not permitted except with a licence.

Copying as a condition of export

7.42   Can films be copied as a condition of export?

Yes. See Section 4.305.

Public administration

7.43   Is copying allowed for public administration purposes?

Yes. See Sections 4.306 and following.

Material open to public inspection.

7.44   Do the rules for public inspection apply to films?

Yes. See Sections 4.310 and following.

Publication right

7.45   Are films subject to publication right?

Yes, in the same way as other works. See Section 4 for more details.

Multimedia

7.46   If a publication contains material in several different forms such as a booklet, computer program and DVD, how is the copyright worked out?

The copyright subsists separately in each item and the rules for that format apply.

So the copyright in the entire package could run out at several different times, like the copyright in a periodical issue. It may also be a database (see Section 9).

7.47   Who is the author of a mixed-media package?

The rules for ownership and authorship are the same as for each of the components. However, the publisher almost certainly owns copyright in the format of the whole package.

7.48   Presumably performers have rights in films just like sound recordings?

The rights are the same but they last for 50 years from the end of the year in which the performance took place or first release of the recording of the performance, unless this recording is a sound recording (see Section 6). If the recording is purely visual then the 50-year rule applies.

Disabled people

7.49 Is it permissible to make copies of films and DVDs in alternative formats for disabled people?

Yes, the same rules apply as for other formats. See Section 4 for details.

Section 8
Broadcasts

See also Section 6 on sound recordings and Section 7 on films.

Definition

8.1   What is the definition of a broadcast?

The definition of a broadcast is 'an electronic transmission of visual images, sounds or other information which is transmitted for simultaneous reception by members of the public and is capable of lawfully being received by them or is transmitted at a time determined solely by the person making the transmission for presentation to members of the public'.

8.2   What about the content of the broadcast?

This is protected quite separately. For example, a modern play is broadcast on radio or TV. The copyright in the play and the performing rights of the actors are all treated separately but the electronic signal that carries the programme attracts rights as a broadcast.

8.3   Some people used to say that websites were broadcasting. Is this still true?

No. The law specifically states that any internet transmission is excluded from the definition of a broadcast unless it is:

- a transmission taking place simultaneously on the internet and by other means
- a concurrent transmission of a live event
- a transmission of recorded moving images or sounds forming part of a programme service offered by the person responsible for making the transmission, and is part of a service transmitted at scheduled times determined by that person.

This is rather wordy so some examples might help. A film is being shown on TV and simultaneously can be watched on your PC via the internet; a horse race can be watched on both TV and via the internet on your PC; a website is designed so that you can view and listen to items on it only at times fixed by the website manager. In all these cases transmission is considered as a broadcast, not internet transmission. As mentioned in Section 4, in a nutshell, broadcasting takes precedence over internet transmission when determining the status of a transmitted work.

8.4   What about services where you can listen to a programme later on rather than when actually transmitted?

Services such as BBC iPlayer are not broadcasts as such, but the content of them is protected as copyright works which have been communicated to the public by electronic means.

8.5   Are cable programme services included?

Yes, a cable programme service can fit the definition of a broadcast. However, if it is an on-demand cable service then the comments in Section 8.4 above apply.

Authorship

8.6   Who is the author of a broadcast?

Essentially it is the person who transmits the programme if that person has any responsibility for its contents.

8.7   Does the author enjoy moral rights?

No.

Ownership of copyright

8.8   Who owns the copyright in a broadcast?

Usually the person who transmits the programme.

8.9   What about a broadcast which includes a record or a film?

There are separate copyrights in the broadcast and the sound recording included in it. In the same way, a television programme which includes a film has separate copyrights in the television transmission and the film in the programme. This is similar to typographical copyright.

8.10   As broadcasts often come from many different countries, which one is regarded as the original?

The country where the uninterrupted signal started is regarded as the country of origin.

8.11   Supposing it is a satellite broadcast?

Legislation makes it clear that where the satellite is merely a re-transmission point it has no significance in determining where the broadcast came from.

Owners' rights

8.12   What rights do owners of copyright in broadcasts have?

Owners have the same rights as in literary, dramatic and musical works. See Section 3. Copying and issuing copies to the public are covered by recording – see below in this section.

Performing, playing or showing a work

8.13   How do these rights work for broadcasts?

Allowing a broadcast to be heard or listened to by members of the public requires a licence from the PRS for Music. This includes shops, offices, hotels (even in the lifts!), restaurants, staffrooms and canteens. See Section 6 for details.

Communicating the work to the public right

8.14   How does the right of communicating the work to the public by electronic means fit in?

By making a broadcast of any work, not only is a broadcast created, but the right of communicating the work to the public is also brought into play. So to broadcast anything requires the consent of the copyright owner. Similarly, putting anything on the internet is also an act requiring the permission of the copyright owner.

Lending and rental

8.15   How does lending and rental work with broadcasts?

Although this may not seem relevant to broadcasts, copies of broadcasts which may be lent must be considered as copies of those broadcasts, even though they also constitute sound recordings or films. In educational establishments, lending of recordings made under Educational Recording Agency (ERA) and Open University (OU) licences (see Section 10) may be restricted. Copies made under the legislation may be transmitted to persons outside the premises of the establishment only through secure electronic networks. It is only possible to rent with the copyright owner's explicit consent.

Publication right

8.16   Is publication right relevant to broadcasts?

This is not relevant to broadcasts.

Duration of copyright

8.17   When does the copyright in a broadcast expire?

Copyright in a broadcast expires 50 years after the year when the broadcast was made.

8.18   What about repeats?

The fact that a programme was repeated does not extend or renew the copyright. A repeat broadcast of a broadcast already out of copyright does not produce a new copyright.

Exceptions

8.19   Is copying for private use allowed for broadcasts?

Yes, but it is covered differently in the law. You may make an off-air recording of a broadcast for purely personal or domestic use but it must not be further copied. See below for details of off-air recording.

Fair dealing

8.20   Is there fair dealing in broadcasts?

Broadcasts are subject to fair dealing like other works. See Section 4 for details.

8.21   **Supposing I want to record something because I am out and will miss it or it clashes with another programme I want to watch or hear?**

Copying from the radio or television for personal use to listen or view at a more convenient time is allowed, provided that the copy is used only for private purposes and the copying is done on your own domestic premises. This is technically called 'time-shifting'. Most TV channels provide facilities for doing this anyway through catch-up services, although these often have time limits on them after which they cannot be accessed.

8.22   **Supposing I ask friends round to watch the recording?**

Provided they are friends or relations and you did not make any charge, this would be legal.

8.23   **Supposing I just want to take a photo of a TV broadcast, perhaps because it has someone I know on it?**

A single copy of an image from a broadcast for private and domestic use is allowed but it must not be further copied or put on a social media website.

Text and data mining

8.24   **Can broadcasts be copied for obtaining information for computational analysis?**

The provisions for text and data mining apply to broadcasts just like any other material.

Educational copying

8.25   **Can broadcasts be used for teaching purposes?**

Yes. A broadcast can be used to illustrate instruction provided the use is fair dealing and the usual restrictions apply, namely that the use is for a non-commercial purpose, the use is by a person giving or receiving instruction, and the source is acknowledged.

8.26 **Some suppliers insist that educational copying of a broadcast received through their system is not allowed. Are they permitted to do this?**

It used to be, but the law is clear that any contract which purports to restrict acts allowed under this area of copyright law is null and void.

8.27 **What is the difference between using a broadcast to illustrate teaching and copying for educational purposes?**

Using a broadcast for the purposes of illustrating instruction does not necessarily mean copying the work. Presumably it includes live transmission within a teaching environment as well as recording for activities such as cutting small extracts, comparing different techniques of, say, newscasting and similar purposes. Educational copying is intended for an educational establishment to make a recording of a broadcast to use in a variety of teaching contexts and retain that permanently.

8.28 **Can broadcasts be copied for classroom use?**

This must be done either with the appropriate licence or under the law as described below. Such licences are now generally available for educational establishments. See Section 10. One exception is when broadcasts are used for training in the making of films or film soundtracks and then only by the teacher or student themselves. But broadcasts can be played or viewed by a class as they are transmitted. Note that the educational establishment can only record broadcasts under these terms if there is no licence. The establishment is required to know that such licences exist and the terms of such licences.

8.29 **Are all broadcasts licensed?**

No. The Educational Recording Agency (ERA) licenses educational establishments to copy broadcasts from BBC, ITV and Channel 5, and the OU issues licences for its own broadcasts. The licences do not cover material from other cable or satellite broadcasts or broadcasts from outside the UK. These broadcasts may be freely recorded as the law states that where no licence is offered recording is legitimate for educational use. BBC and ITV also have various licences, such as in the BBC Creative Archive licence, which allow free use for non-commercial educational purposes.

8.30 **Are there any restrictions?**

If you copy under an ERA or OU licence you must observe the limits of that licence.

Other copying is subject to the following conditions:

* The source of the broadcast must be acknowledged.
* The educational purpose must be non-commercial.
* The copy of the broadcast must not be transmitted to any person outside the premises of the establishment except through a secure electronic network.

8.31 Can recordings of these broadcasts be lent or transmitted to students?

This depends on the location of the student to whom the recording is transmitted (which presumably includes lending). Such broadcasts must not be transmitted to people off the premises, except through a secure electronic network. They may also be made available through dedicated terminals on the premises provided that this does not conflict with any contracts or agreements under which access to them was agreed.

8.32 What about podcasts and similar services?

Because these can be viewed at times chosen by the viewer they are not legally broadcasts, but it is important to check the terms of any licences to see whether they are included.

8.33 Does this mean that organisations that are not considered educational can make off-air recordings?

No, the provisions and the licences apply only to educational establishments.

Library and archive copying

8.34 Can libraries and archives record off-air for their collections?

Yes. Qualifying libraries and archives can make off-air recordings and add them to their collections. See Section 4.195 for details of qualifying libraries.

8.35 Can these recordings be lent to other libraries?

Yes, in the same way as other works. See Section 4 for details.

8.36 Can they be copied for preservation?

Again, the answer is yes, with the usual restrictions. See Section 4.

8.37   **Can recordings of broadcasts be made for disabled people in appropriate formats?**

Yes, provided the conditions set out in Section 4 are observed. See Sections 4.326 and following for details.

8.38   **Can archives keep off-air recordings made for 'time-shifting' purposes?**

No. They must be kept and used by the person who made them for their own use. Copies made under the ERA licences are a different matter and can be kept indefinitely. OU broadcasts usually have conditions relating to the period they are kept. Notification of this time limit set by the OU is attached to them.

Section 9
Databases

Definition

9.1 What is the definition of a database?

A database is defined as: 'a collection of works, data or other materials which:

- are arranged in a systematic or methodical way, and
- are individually accessible by electronic or other means'.

9.2 Are databases protected by copyright?

Databases can certainly be subject to copyright but they are also subject to a quite separate database right.

9.3 Can a literary work also be a database?

Yes, it can. In order to be recognised as a literary work, a database will be eligible only if it is original (a vital test for copyright protection) and the selection of the contents and arrangement of the database constitutes the author's own intellectual creation. In this case the database will acquire copyright protection. The courts have also ruled that if a database is the work of an individual but that person was acting under strict instructions then the work does not qualify for copyright, only database right.

9.4 Must a database be electronic to be protected?

Definitely not. The phrase 'other means' makes that very clear. Databases in paper or audio format, for example, are also protected.

Copyright and database right

9.5   Are all databases protected by database right?

All modern ones will be, but some databases which are quite old (established before 1983) qualify only for copyright under the term 'compilation' (see Section 4.24 for compilations).

9.6   How does something qualify for database right?

To qualify for database right the contents of the database must have been assembled as the result of substantial investment in obtaining, verifying or presenting the contents.

9.7   Does investment just mean money?

No. Investment specifically includes financial, human or technical resources.

9.8   Does 'obtain' mean you must get the data from somewhere else?

Yes, and this is a vital point about databases. It has been ruled that in order to claim database right you must obtain the data. Obtaining means that it already exists. Anyone who creates a database from scratch cannot claim database right, only copyright.

Example: Someone makes a list of retail outlets in a town (see Section 9.29). This forms a database and qualifies because the person making the list obtained the data about the shops. Someone else plans a calendar of events for the village choral society. This cannot be a database because the person planning the calendar did not obtain the data but created it and, until that person chose the events, that data did not exist.

9.9   If the database is made up of material which is not copyright, is the database still protected?

Yes, if it qualifies as a database. The copyright status of the content of a database is irrelevant. It is the construction of the database that is the key question.

9.10   Can anyone use non-copyright material included in a database?

Yes, provided they do not extract a substantial part of the database and they are not prevented from doing so by contract or licence. The exceptions detailed in Section 4, which cannot be overridden by contract, do not apply to database right.

9.11   Supposing out-of-copyright material is collected from a number of databases, as permitted, and then organised into a new database. Does this also qualify for database right?

Yes, because the data has been obtained and then verified and presented.

Authorship

9.12   Who is the author of a database?

Apart from the fairly rare occasion when a database has a personal author (see Section 9.3), the author is defined as the maker of the database. The maker of a database is the person who takes the initiative in obtaining, verifying or presenting the contents of the database and assumes the risk of investing in those actions and therefore obtains the database right. Makers cannot qualify for this right unless they are individuals with EEA nationality, or companies/organisations incorporated within the EEA, or partnerships or unincorporated bodies formed under the law of an EEA state.

9.13   Are there moral rights in databases?

There are no moral rights in databases unless they are the creation of an individual person, when the usual rules about derogatory treatment would apply.

Ownership of copyright and database right

9.14   Who is the owner of database right?

Where copyright subsists, the copyright rules apply (see Section 3). Ownership of database right belongs to the maker of the database, although the usual rules about ownership of works made as part of employment or for the Crown apply.

Duration of copyright and database right

9.15   How long do the rights in databases last?

When a database attracts copyright protection the usual rules of duration of copyright for literary works apply (see Section 4). When database right applies this lasts for 15 years from the end of the year in which the database was completed. If, during that time, it is made available to the public, then the 15-year term runs from the end of the year in which the database was made available.

9.16 **But databases are constantly being updated. What happens to the length of protection then?**

If substantial changes, including accumulation of data, additions or deletions take place, so that the updated database would be considered the subject of substantial new investment, then the 15-year period will begin again. In other words, where a database is frequently being updated it remains protected by database right for 15 years after the final changes have been made. Only when the database is closed does the 15-year period start to run down.

9.17 **What about old databases?**

Where a database was completed after 1 January 1983 and the database right began to operate when the regulations came into force in 1997, then that database obtains database right until 31 December 2012.

9.18 **What about databases which already exist but which would not qualify for copyright under the new rules?**

If the database was made before 27 March 1996 and was in copyright immediately before the regulations came into force, then it remains in copyright under the usual rules for copyright duration.

Owners' rights

9.19 **What rights does the owner of database right enjoy?**

The rights of database rights owners are defined in a different way from those of copyright owners, as described below.

9.20 **What rights does the owner of database right have?**

The owner of the database right has the right to prevent the extraction or re-utilisation of all or a substantial part of the contents of the database.

9.21 **What precisely does 'extraction' mean?**

The word 'extraction' is defined as 'permanent or temporary transfer of the contents to another medium by any means or in any form'.

9.22 **Does this mean that nothing can ever be taken from a database?**

No. A user is allowed to extract small amounts of data provided that the amount taken is insubstantial.

9.23 **What counts as insubstantial?**

This is not defined, but in deciding if the amount taken is substantial or not, quality and quantity are both factors, separately and together. So it is possible to take a small quantity but still infringe the database right because of the quality of what has been taken. The reverse is also true.

Also the courts have judged that a substantial part of a database must be so large that it would be in competition with the original database from which it was taken. So this might be a very large amount.

9.24 **Supposing someone copies an insubstantial amount one day and then does the same a few days later. Is this allowed?**

No. The law has spotted this cunning ploy. It specifies that systematic extraction of insubstantial parts of a database may amount to extraction of substantial amounts. In other words, extractions done at different times must be seen as cumulative.

9.25 **What about 're-utilisation'? Does this stop me using any information?**

No. 'Re-utilisation' is defined as 'making the contents available to the public by any means'. Re-utilisation is dealt with under 'Fair dealing'.

9.26 **Surely this is making facts subject to copyright?**

Not really. Copyright and the other rights associated with it refer to using someone else's property. Imagine someone has compiled a list of ice-cream makers in east coast resorts. There is nothing to stop someone else compiling their own list and issuing this as a free or commercial product, provided they have compiled it from scratch and not used the other person's list. The idea behind database right is to give some protection to the person who invested in putting the data together in the first place, to give them exclusive control not over those facts but over the way those facts have been assembled and made available.

9.27 **What about other rights, such as copying, issuing to the public and so on?**

These are really covered by the right to prevent extraction and re-utilisation. If you cannot extract then you cannot do any of the things a copyright owner would have the exclusive right to do anyway. Other rights such as performance, publication right or making available right would not apply to databases.

Exceptions

Copying for private use

9.28   Can databases be copied for private use?

No. But copying for personal use of small parts of a database is permitted as detailed in 'fair dealing' (below).

Fair dealing

9.29   Are databases subject to fair dealing in the same way as literary works?

Yes, but with an important difference. Where a database is *copyright* then it is subject to fair dealing for research for a non-commercial purpose or private study provided the source is indicated. Where the database is subject only to *database right* then the following rules apply.

First, if you need to use a substantial part of the database, you can do this provided that it is for non-commercial research or private study and the source is acknowledged where possible. So you can certainly look up the addresses of the five or six ice-cream manufacturers in Bridlington and Scarborough and write them down for your own use, but this information cannot be issued to the public in the form of a trade directory or database, or in any other way. Whether you need to write down on your piece of paper by the telephone the source of the information to comply with this rule seems highly unlikely! Second, if the amount taken is insubstantial and you are a lawful user of the database you can extract *and* re-utilise this information, but not re-package it for publication or further use. But remember that 'insubstantial amounts' is not defined and the amount will vary according to the nature of the database and the material extracted.

9.30   Why is commercial research excluded?

The law is specific that *anything* done to a database for the purposes of research for a commercial purpose is not fair dealing with that database.

9.31   Is there a definition of 'commercial'?

No, but any use which will bring commercial benefit to an organisation or individual would be considered as commercial.

9.32   What constitutes a lawful user?

A lawful user is someone who has a right to use the database. In a paper context this is anyone entitled to use the library where it is stored, or any private owner of a database or anyone they permit to have access to it. In the electronic context it is anyone who legitimately has a licence to use or be allowed to use the database.

9.33 Are users of library services lawful users?

This depends on the licence the library has with the database owner. For electronic databases it is important to ensure the library's licence includes as wide a range of users as possible so that nobody is excluded. For commercial companies lawful users may be a much more restricted group (e.g. company employees only, or even only those in the research and development department).

9.34 Some electronic databases come with very strict licences. Can these prevent any use of the database at all?

Not legally. The terms of any contract that aims to prevent a lawful user from extracting or re-utilising insubstantial parts of the database will be considered null and void in law.

Text and data mining

9.35 Do the rules on text and data mining apply to databases?

Despite the title, text and data mining is not permitted in the same way as for other works. Copying of the contents of a database is governed by the rules mentioned above and not by those for other works.

9.36 Why does text and data mining not apply to databases?

Because it is an exception to copyright and not to database right.

Educational copying

9.37 Can databases be copied for educational purposes?

Where a database is protected only by copyright then the usual rules apply. Where database right exists then this is not infringed if a substantial part is extracted for the purposes of illustration for teaching or research, this is not done for any commercial purpose, and the source is acknowledged.

9.38 Does this mean material can be extracted to illustrate research?

This is not at all clear. Whether 'illustration' belongs with 'teaching' or 'teaching and research' is not stated. With copyright works, copying is allowed to illustrate teaching but this does not necessarily mean the same interpretation should be given here. The words given are those from the law — only a judge may ever sort this out!

Library and archive copying

9.39 Can databases be made available through libraries?

Essentially the answer is 'yes'. Certainly under a licence from the database owner this can be done, but it is essential to ensure that all legitimate users of the library are designated as 'lawful users', otherwise they do not have the right to use any of the material in the database. If the database is in paper format, problems of access do not arise in database right terms, but the issue of what users may copy remains.

9.40 Can libraries copy parts of databases for users?

Where a database is copyright (only) then libraries may copy as they can other library works (a reasonable proportion); however, library copying is not permitted for database right, so the abilities of libraries to copy in this respect are limited to copying an insubstantial part.

9.41 Can databases be copied for preservation and replacement?

Not under the rules described for other materials, although making a paper copy of an existing paper database might be a reasonable action if the rules are strictly observed.

Other restrictions

Adaptation

9.42 Supposing someone took a database, altered the way it was arranged and then re-issued it?

This is not allowed as the law specifically defines adaptation as including arrangement or alteration of the version or translation.

Lending and rental

9.43 **Presumably libraries cannot lend databases?**

Yes, they can. It is easy to think that database = electronic database, but these rules apply to paper copies too. So, the lending of a database is not considered as extraction or re-utilisation and is therefore allowed under the same conditions as literary works. Similarly on-the-spot reference is permitted. However, public libraries cannot lend databases, as they are not covered by PLR. As with all materials, rental is prohibited without the specific consent of the rights owner.

Making copies available for public inspection

9.44 **Can databases be made available for public inspection?**

Similar rules to those for literary works apply to databases.

Public administration

9.45 **Can databases be copied for the purposes of public administration?**

Similar rules to those for literary works apply to databases.

Disabled people

9.46 **Can databases be made available in alternative formats for disabled people?**

Yes, database right is not infringed by making an accessible copy of a work, as set out in Section 4.323 and following.

Section 10
Licensing schemes and licences

10.1 How do licensing schemes and licences work?

The situation relating to licensing schemes and licences is changing all the time. This section simply outlines the major schemes and licences, how they work, and what benefits and limitations they bring. Details of individual licensing schemes need to be obtained from the relevant agency or organisation. Details of appropriate websites and addresses are given in 'Useful sources of information'. The outline information in this chapter is current as at summer 2019.

10.2 What is the difference between a licensing scheme and a licence?

A licensing scheme covers a defined range of works and is offered to a particular class of organisation (for example, government departments, academic institutions), which anyone who is in the class named can join. A licence is more often an agreement between the copyright owner and an individual user. Their terms may be similar to a licensing scheme but are usually tailored to the specific needs of the user.

Licensing schemes
10.3 What is a licensing scheme?

It is a scheme that allows someone who is not the copyright owner to use copyright material beyond the limits of the law with the permission of the copyright owner, which is obtained through a licence issued by an organisation on behalf of the copyright owner.

10.4 Who administers such schemes?

They are administered by different organisations, which can change. They are briefly described in the following paragraphs. In addition copyright owners can, and do, issue their own independent licences. These may be 'one-off' owners of copyright or large organisations such as the BBC or OS.

10.5   Are licensing schemes relevant to libraries?

Certainly, because any licence held by the organisation that owns or administers the library may include copying carried out in the library or by library staff. But it is unusual for licensing schemes to be only for the library. The library is part of a larger organisation, which is licensed as a whole.

10.6   Do libraries have to abide by the rules of such licences?

Yes. They represent a contract between the licensing agency and the licensee.

10.7   What are the details of such schemes?

Each scheme varies according to the type of material covered and the type of organisation holding the licence. The terms and conditions of licences vary from one type of organisation to another and from time to time, so anything said here about the terms of a licence should be checked with the licensing agency before a licence is considered. These notes are for general guidance only. Note too that a licence is a contract and the terms of the contract are what count in the end, not advice or comments in a general book on copyright such as this one!

10.8   How do licences work with exceptions such as fair dealing, library privilege and education?

Essentially the licence is there to permit copying or use beyond what the law permits. Any clauses in a licence that prohibit the exercise of rights given to users by Parliament are automatically null and void.

10.9   What about copying materials from other countries?

Some agencies have agreements with a number of countries to collect royalties on behalf of copyright owners in those countries. Check with the relevant licensing agency, as their coverage is constantly expanding.

10.10   What are the major licensing agencies and schemes?

The brief description below gives a general idea of each agency and the type of licence it offers. Specific details should be obtained from the appropriate agency.

10.11   The Copyright Licensing Agency (CLA)

The CLA is owned jointly by the societies representing authors and publishers. It is the largest agency that libraries encounter. It offers a range of licences to copy onto and from paper and also offers a licence for scanning from a wide variety of media. Some licences allow the making of scanned copies and putting them onto a secure intranet site as well as copying and storing from electronic 'born digital' material, although this latter facility is optional for the publisher. Again, see the CLA website for details. The CLA has an agreement with the Design and Artists Copyright Society (DACS), so the CLA can offer a licence which includes the copying of artistic works embedded in text items as well. Note that the CLA rather than the Newspaper Licensing Agency (NLA, see Sections 10.19–21) licenses the copying of a number of popular magazines for educational purposes. Check the website for details of titles. There is also a Schools Printed Music Licence, which allows a wide range of copying and creative uses of printed music.

These are the main areas covered by the CLA:

- *Educational copying*: The licence allows one copy of one article from a periodical issue or 5% of a book or one chapter; one copy for each pupil in a class and one for the teacher, whether school, college or university. Some websites can also be copied under this licence. Libraries may also be allowed to make one copy of such material for the short-loan collection. Separate licences currently exist for local education authority schools, independent schools, further education colleges and higher education institutions. As details vary, consult the CLA website for details. The CLA now has a licence negotiated with the Department for Education whereby individual state-funded schools and authorities do not need to negotiate separate licences but are covered by one from central government.
- *Government departments*: Licences are structured according to the needs of the department.
- *Industry and commerce*: A model licence was negotiated with the Confederation of British Industry, which it could recommend to its members (but could not negotiate for them). This is in the form of a matrix consisting of the sector in which the company operates and the number of research staff they employ. A similar licence has been negotiated for legal firms with the Law Society. There is also a special licence for regulatory material required by the pharmaceutical industry. Other sectors include media organisations, and hotel and conference venues. These licences often include

scanning UK publications and putting the image onto a secure intranet site There is also a 'plus' licence which links the services provided by the British Library.

Other licences for different sectors are continually being offered and negotiated.

The CLA website has a very extensive list of the types of licence available and their scope. Visit www.cla.co.uk and click on 'licences'.

10.12 Does the CLA licence cover copying for disabled people?

The CLA licence includes the making of copies in any format necessary to enable a disabled person to access material not otherwise available in a suitable format, although the law now gives disabled people the right to have copies made in any format necessary for them to be able to use the item concerned.

10.13 What about providing copies to people outside my organisation?

The CLA currently (summer 2019) offers three document delivery licences:

- a Transactional Document Delivery Licence
- a Low Volume Document Delivery Licence
- a library licence scheme (known colloquially as the Sticker Scheme).

10.14 What are the differences?

The Transactional Document Delivery Licence allows any library to provide copies of documents for commercial research. It is designed for libraries that deliver more than 100 copies a month for commercial research. Copyright fees are set individually by publishers.

The Low Volume Document Delivery Licence is intended for libraries that deliver fewer than 100 copies a month for commercial purposes. The copyright fee is a flat fee.

The Sticker Scheme is intended for libraries that have walk-in users who are not employees or members of the institution, such as people using public libraries or members of the general public using a university library. This scheme is also a flat fee one. The library collects the fee from the user and passes it to the CLA with bibliographic details of the works covered; the CLA eventually raises an invoice for the amount collected. The user attaches a copy of the form to the photocopy to show it is legitimate.

10.15   Why can't an employee of a company with a CLA licence simply go into a public library and make a copy under the firm's licence?

The CLA licence only covers material, copies of which are owned by the organisation holding the licence. So anything in the public library, of which the company did not own its own copy, could not be covered by the company's own licence.

10.16   Why can't they be made under the licence held by the local authority or university?

Copies cannot be made under the licence held by the local authority or university because the CLA licence allows copying only by employees or consultants working for the organisation holding the licence. So the reader in a public library or visitor to a university library cannot be covered by this licence either.

10.17   Many journals have details of payment to the Copyright Clearance Center (CCC) in the USA printed on the bottom of the page. Must libraries pay these fees to the CCC?

Payment should be made only if copies are made beyond what UK law permits. The CLA currently acts as the agent for the CCC and they should be contacted in cases of doubt. The national copyright agencies work together to form an international network through which payments are transferred.

10.18   Christian Copyright Licensing International (CCLI)

CCLI offers a licence for the copying of the words and music of many hymns. Licences are available for churches, schools and conference centres but the original work must be owned by the licensee. Borrowing copies from a library outside the licensed organisation and then copying is not covered by the licence. CCLI also administers a scheme to allow churches, societies and clubs to play sound recordings at meetings where appropriate. CCLI also acts as an agent for the CLA, providing a licence for the copying of non-music material such as books and magazines for discussion groups and other areas where multiple copies might be needed.

10.19   The Newspaper Licensing Agency (NLA)

Unlike the CLA, the NLA is wholly owned by the newspaper publishing industry. The NLA offers a range of licences to different sectors. There is a standard copying licence but separate terms. Currently the licence covers all national and the vast majority of regional newspapers as well as newspapers from a number of overseas publishers. Check the NLA website for details. Note that a number of popular magazines are now licensed for education through the CLA. See www.cla.co.uk for details.

10.20   What does the NLA licence allow?

The NLA licence allows:

- photocopying, faxing and digital reproduction of press cuttings
- copying for internal management purposes
- copying for educational purposes
- in certain cases, copying to members and clients.

There are also licences for charities, public relations companies, corporate website republishing and website end-users.

10.21   Can someone with an NLA licence copy material in other libraries?

Yes. Unlike the CLA licence the NLA licence covers the copying of all the newspapers licensed, regardless of whether the licensee owns a copy of them or not.

10.22   The Design and Artists Copyright Society (DACS)

DACS offers an individual service to obtain permission to use an artist's work in any context from publishing images in books or on the internet to using them for advertising or even fabric design. Collective licences for photocopying are negotiated through the CLA and for broadcasting on TV through ERA.

10.23   The Educational Recording Agency (ERA)

ERA offers a licence for educational establishments only for off-air recording of broadcasts (TV and radio) from all scheduled free-to-air radio and television broadcasts.

As there is no licence for other cable or satellite broadcasting at present, these programmes may be freely recorded for educational purposes, unless the contract for receiving these services explicitly excludes recording for educational purposes, which some contracts do. Once recorded, a copy may be used for teaching and further copied within the terms of the licence. It may be kept in the library of the institution for which it was recorded. Licensed items must be labelled as such and may be lent only in exceptional circumstances within the terms of the ERA licence. Recording does not have to be done on the premises – it could be carried out by a teacher or lecturer at home for subsequent use within the licensed premises. The ERA digital licence permits the streaming of broadcasts to eligible students but only within the licensed premises.

Note that the BBC and ITV have issued notices to allow educational establishments to record online services such as iPlayer under their ERA licence. Further details can be found at www.bbc.co.uk or www.itv.com or www.channel4.com.

10.24   Some cable or satellite services put conditions in their licences which prohibit the recording of broadcasts for educational purposes. Is this legal?

Not now. Where any clause in a licence or contract purports to override the privileges given by Parliament, that clause is considered null and void.

10.25   Open University Educational Enterprises

The Open University used to license its material separately but OU broadcasts and TV programmes are now covered by the ERA licence.

10.26   Her Majesty's Stationery Office (HMSO)

It is government policy to permit many documents published, or controlled, by HMSO to be freely copied. Most legislation and similar material, and many official reports and documents, can be copied and reused. Single and multiple copies are allowed and documents may be included in other works (such as textbooks), and they can be included in websites and other publications. In addition, material classed as public records (see Section 4.319) may be freely copied, republished, included in books and journal articles, used as the basis for making a broadcast or film, indexed or translated without payment of any fee. The source of the document must be acknowledged and its integrity respected and the institution holding the document may charge the fees necessary to cover the costs of providing the document.

The Royal Coat of Arms may not be included in copying as this has become a sort of trademark or guarantee of integrity.

As this is a rapidly changing area, it is best to consult the HMSO website for the latest guidance. See www.nationalarchives.gov.uk/doc/open-government-licence/version/3/.

10.27   Ordnance Survey (OS)

OS has introduced a wide range of licences for education, local authorities, commercial and business, legal procedures and planning permissions. They are very detailed and liable to radical change from time to time and it would be misleading to describe them all here. The most important one for the general public and public libraries is that OS allows a library to supply copies or a member of the public to make copies up to the following limits: four copies may be made provided they are from a single map and that no more than 625 cm2 (A4 size) are made, and this is at the original size – no enlargements are allowed. Although OS is no longer Crown copyright, maps produced more than 50 years ago are still out of copyright as Crown copyright in artistic works expires 50 years after creation and the new status of OS does not affect the status of these maps.

There are separate schemes for local authority and planning applications and libraries are advised not to get involved in copying for these purposes as they may not be aware of the finer points of the agreement.

Details of educational, commercial and other types of licence should be obtained from OS direct. Note that OS has stated it is content for readers to use digital cameras when copying for themselves.

10.28   The British Standards Institution

The British Standards Institution no longer issues special licences for classroom use. Terms and conditions for using standards can be found at www.bsigroup.com/en-GB/about-bsi/legal/intellectual-property-notice/ (consulted 6 September 2018).

10.29   British Phonographic Industry

Libraries may not lend sound recordings except under licence, and such a licence has been negotiated by CILIP with British Phonographic Industry for public libraries (only). This is based on a combination of the number of copies of any one work held at any one service point and a 'holdback' period for new releases when they will not be lent. There is no licence fee.

10.30   PRS for Music (formerly the Performing Right Society and the Mechanical Copyright Protection Society)

PRS for Music is one of the oldest licensing societies in the world. It licenses all public performances of music, whether these are live or recorded, including public use of radios and television. Any playing of music for public reception needs a licence. This includes playing a radio or showing a TV programme as well as music transmitted over the internet. PRS for Music also licenses the recording of music onto any medium and re-recording of music from abroad.

10.31   The Public Video Screening Licence

This licence has been created by Filmbank Media to represent major Hollywood and many independent Bollywood film companies. Filmbank offers a licence to schools, educational organisations and clubs for showing films within its repertoire. It also offers licences to business and entertainment locations for background screening.

10.32   The Mechanical Copyright Protection Society (MCPS)

MCPS has merged with The Performing Right Society. See Section 10.30 above.

10.33   Phonographic Performance Ltd (PPL)

PPL is a music industry collecting society representing over 2500 record companies, from the large multinationals to the small independents. It collects licence fees from broadcast and public performance users on behalf of the record companies. This licence fee revenue, after deduction of running costs, is then distributed to the record company members and performers. Libraries and others should note that when a recording containing music is played in public then royalties are due to both PRS and PPL, as one collects for the composers and musicians and the other for the recording company. This now includes churches, clubs and societies that are charities.

10.34   The Motion Picture Licensing Corporation (MPLC)

MPLC licenses the public performance of motion pictures. It represents over 80 producers and distributors and includes most major Hollywood studios, as well as many independent ones. Any public performance requires a licence, including educational establishments, when the material is not being used for instruction (see Sections 6.51–54). Note that nurseries and pre-school groups are not included in the definition of an educational establishment. There is also now a licence for hotels and letting rooms.

10.35   The Music Publishers Association

Although the Music Publishers Association is not a licensing body it has negotiated some specific permissions, including some educational copying, through the CLA. There is also a special permission for copying music for adjudicators in festivals such as those organised by the British and International Federation of Festivals.

10.36 **What about other licences?**

There is an increasingly bewildering array of licences and permissions systems available. Many individual publishers have their own tailor-made licences for different situations. It is impossible here to do more than mention that these exist and users should follow them up as necessary.

An increasing number of documents are now made available to the public via various collaborative online services such as Creative Commons, open access services and open archives.

10.37 **Are there licences for using orphan works?**

The UK Government has a licensing scheme for the use of orphan works outside the usual exceptions. The scheme allows use beyond legal permissions for commercial or non-commercial use in return for fees set by the government. These fees are passed to copyright owners in the event of their being identified. For details go to www.ipo.gov.uk.

Creative Commons

10.38 **What is Creative Commons?**

Creative Commons is probably the best-known alternative method of disseminating academic publications. Creative Commons licenses the copying, reuse, distribution and, in some cases, modification of the original owner's creative work without having to obtain permission every single time from the rights holder. Owners of the rights in documents made available through Creative Commons have to allow most of these uses, otherwise the objective of making documents more freely available is not achieved. Copyright owners tag their documents to show what uses are permitted, using a code system for ease of reference.

10.39 **Can material licensed under Creative Commons be used by anyone?**

Yes, and in any way indicated by the copyright owner.

10.40 **Are these the only ways documents can be used?**

Not necessarily. Contributors to Creative Commons can choose to be more generous and allow, for example, commercial use of their documents. There is even a code which allows the copyright owner to waive all their rights so the material can be used in any way at all.

10.41 **Is this legally binding or could a copyright owner complain about use of the material?**

The Creative Commons licence is considered binding as an agreement in English and Welsh law and as a contract in Scottish law. Provided you stick to the limits set by the copyright owner and observe any conditions, such as acknowledging the source, you are acting legally.

Open archives or access

10.42 **What is open archives or access?**

Open archives or open access is a movement to make scholarly publications more readily available to the academic community. Various models exist. For example, an author may submit a paper for online publication and pay a fee for this. Access to the paper is then free for users, who do not need to subscribe to the conventional journal. Another model is that there is no fee but only those who contribute may gain access to the papers.

10.43 **Does this mean that the papers can be freely copied and distributed?**

No. Unless the copyright owner states to the contrary, the usual restrictions apply.

These are just examples and others can be found and will emerge! However, the questions and answers given here are likely to be valid for any similar service.

Section 11

Computer programs, the electronic world and websites

11.1 What is the difference between electronic material and databases?

It is very important to distinguish between electronic material and databases. One is the format in which a work is stored or transmitted; the other is a form of a work itself. There are many works which are electronic but not databases and equally many databases that are not electronic! This chapter tries to deal with some of these questions but users of this book should realise that this is a constantly changing situation and the subject matter, questions and answers are all moving targets. Because the term 'electronic materials' can cover works in electronic form, computer programs and databases these items will be dealt with separately within the usual headings in this chapter, although they are all linked together in some respects.

11.2 Is copyright very different for electronic materials?

The answers to many copyright questions that arise in the electronic world are exactly the same as those to the questions that arise in the more traditional paper-based world. However, some issues are peculiar to electronic materials and some of the answers which are clear in the paper world are not so obvious when we deal with electronic materials. Many of the exceptions described in other chapters are exceptions to copyright; database right is completely separate and these exceptions do not apply to databases unless they are (rarely) copyright works.

Computer programs

11.3 Are computer programs a separate sort of work?

In some ways but not in others. Although computer programs are classed as literary works, some special conditions apply. They are literary works because the definition of a literary work is that it is 'written, spoken or sung and recorded in some notation or code'. Computer programs are a series of 0s and 1s, so this is a code which is recorded.

11.4 What about computer programs which have been printed out?

These are literary works. See Section 4.

11.5 A lot of work goes into preparing the design of a computer program. Is that protected as well?

The preparatory work would in any case be considered as a literary work, and the law specifies that this type of work is protected.

11.6 Who is the author of a computer program?

The person who wrote the program.

11.7 How long does copyright in a computer program last?

The same as for a literary work (see Section 4).

11.8 What rights does the copyright owner of a computer program have?

Basically, the same as in a literary work (see Section 4).

11.9 Are there any special rules?

In addition to the usual understanding of the word 'translation' it is worth noting that translation of a computer program includes transferring it from one computer language to another. But see Section 11.11.

Private copying

11.10 Is it permitted to copy a computer program for private use?

No, but the making of back-up copies is permitted under a different part of the law. See below.

Fair dealing

11.11 Are computer programs subject to fair dealing?

Yes, but just how this could work in practice is difficult to determine. One area where a sort of fair dealing exists is to allow the translation of a lower-language program into a higher language. Strangely, the law excludes this activity under fair dealing but specifically allows it in another part of the legislation! This sort of translation must be carried out by a lawful user of the program.

11.12 What about making back-up copies?

If a lawful user needs to make a back-up copy for lawful use of the program this is not an infringement of copyright. 'Lawful use' is not defined.

11.13 Supposing a programmer wants to use the program to create a completely separate program? Can the program be decompiled for this purpose?

Yes, provided that the necessary conditions are met. These are that the information obtained through decompiling the program is not used for any other purpose than creating an independent program, which must not be similar to the one decompiled. In addition the information must not be passed on to anyone, unless that person needs to know it for the purposes of creating the new program, nor must the information be readily available through any other source.

11.14 Sometimes contracts forbid some of the copying outlined in the previous paragraphs. Can anything be done?

Yes, the law specifically states that where a contract tries to prevent any of these actions then that element of the contract is null and void.

11.15 Communication to the public by electronic means

Putting any computer program onto the internet without the copyright owner's explicit consent is an infringement.

Lending and rental

11.16 Can computer programs be lent or rented out?

They can be lent, other than by public libraries, but cannot be rented without the copyright owner's consent. See Sections 4.72–73.

Translation and adaptation

11.17   Is this right relevant to computer programs?

Yes. A clause in the law allows the translation of a lower-language program into a higher language.

Educational copying

11.18   Can computer programs be copied for educational purposes?

The rules for using copyright works for the purposes of illustration when providing or receiving instruction apply to computer programs. See Section 4 for details. Some software is made available specifically for educational purposes and is free of copyright restrictions, provided it is not exploited for commercial purposes.

Library and archive copying

11.19   Can computer programs be copied by libraries and archives for their users?

Theoretically this is possible, although it would be difficult to determine what a reasonable proportion of a computer program is. If this is possible it could then be copied for the reader as part of a non-periodical work (see Sections 4.219 and following, and especially 4.221.

11.20   What happens if the library has a computer program or other electronic material which becomes unusable for technical reasons? Can it be copied so that it can continue to be used?

Yes, this could be justified as preservation or replacement. Any clause in a contract or licence which purports to prohibit this is null and void.

Electronic materials

11.21   Are electronic materials defined in legal terms?

Yes. 'electronic' means actuated by electric, magnetic, electromagnetic, electro-chemical or electromechanical energy, and 'in electronic form' means in a form usable only by electronic means.

11.22   Are electronic materials a separate group of protected works?

No. What is protected is the content of the electronic material and the electronic version of it. This is just like a paper copy where the contents of a book and the typography are protected separately.

11.23 But electronic materials always need some software to make them work. Is this part of the copyright in the work?

No. It is important to distinguish between the content of the work and the supporting computer systems. The latter are copyright in their own right as computer software. For example, it would be possible to have an electronic document which was out of copyright, but software which was still protected.

11.24 Are e-mails protected by copyright?

If the message meets the criteria for being eligible for copyright (original, fixed and from an appropriate country), it is capable of being protected. Straightforward business messages merely confirming details of a contract or specification are probably not protected, nor are short personal messages such as 'meet me at the pub for lunch', but messages that contain opinion or some form of original wording certainly are protected.

11.25 Can e-mails be sent on to other people?

Only if the person who sent it says so, or it is generally understood to be the practice in the organisation. While it is probably acceptable to send an e-mail message to someone else in the same organisation as the person to whom it was sent, it certainly is not allowed to send it to an outside organisation or person.

11.26 What about scanned copies of original documents?

These copies may be copyright, depending on the technology used. If the scanned file is no more than an electronic photocopy and cannot be manipulated it is unlikely to attract copyright. But if more sophisticated software is used it may attract copyright. See Section 2.6 for more details.

Computer-generated works

11.27 Some works are generated automatically by computer, so who is the author of a computer-generated work?

The law says it is the person by whom the arrangements necessary for the creation of the work were undertaken.

11.28   Is it really possible for a work to be totally computer-generated?

This is open to debate. Although there are documents which can be generated automatically, somewhere along the line a human person set up the program to generate the work or at least gave the computer some instructions on how this should be done subsequently.

11.29   How long does the copyright in a computer-generated work last?

The copyright in a computer-generated work expires 50 years from the end of the year in which the work was made.

Authorship of electronic materials

11.30   Who is the author of an electronic work?

The author of the content of an electronic work is decided in the same way as if that work were not electronic: if it is an electronic text, think of it as a book or periodical article; if it is a picture, consider whether it is a photograph or painting, and so on.

Moral rights

11.31   Do authors of electronic materials enjoy moral rights?

Yes, in exactly the same way as they enjoy moral rights of other materials. However, the internet may be used to create artistic works where authors have the right to have their name attached to a work when exhibited in public. Moral rights are very important in an electronic context. It is very easy to change content or authorship, or conceal the origin of a work in an electronic context, and all of these moral rights are enjoyed by authors. Essentially the same rules apply as for the paper world.

11.32   If the work is scanned or digitised who is the author of the electronic version?

It is unlikely that the scanned or digitised version of a work will have an individual author. Unless one can specifically be identified, the electronic version is considered anonymous and the rules for anonymous works apply. See Sections 4.105 and 4.17.

11.33 Does authorship really matter in electronic documents?

Yes, and it will become a vital issue. Researchers and users generally want to know who was responsible for a document, database or any other work, as this has a bearing on its importance and value. It also gives an idea of the point of view behind an author's work. It is also possible to use technology to link authorship to payment. Anyway, those who write really do want the credit, even if there is no money involved.

Ownership

11.34 What are the rules for ownership of electronic works?

The same as for materials in printed format.

Owners' rights

11.35 Do owners enjoy the same rights for electronic materials as they do for paper materials?

Broadly yes, but with some very important additions and one or two changes, as outlined below.

11.36 Who has the right to copy the work?

This is an exclusive right of the owner.

11.37 But surely every use of an electronic document, especially via the web, involves copying? Does this mean that all such copying is an infringement?

Fortunately not. Although such copies are copyright, the legislation prevents the copyright owner from enforcing copyright in such temporary copies provided that:

- they are a necessary part of the technical process to transfer the information
- the transfer is between third parties (website→ISP→end-user)
- the intended use is otherwise legal
- the temporary copy does not have any independent economic significance.

11.38 What would constitute a copy with economic significance?

The law does not say, but if you send someone a fax and the person receiving it prints it out immediately then the intermediate digital copies are not significant. But if the recipient stored the message so it could be re-transmitted to lots of other people in their organisation that would certainly have an independent economic significance.

11.39   Who has the right to issue copies to the public?

This is an exclusive right of the copyright owner and needs to be interpreted in the context of physical carriers such as CD-ROMs or DVDs.

11.40   Who has the right to perform, show or play the work?

These rights are the same as for literary works. Be aware that allowing something to be viewed by a number of people all at the same time is considered a performance and viewing by more than one person at a time is sometimes prohibited under some licences for electronic materials.

11.41   Who has the right to adapt or translate the work?

These rights are the same as for literary works.

Lending and rental

11.42   Can electronic materials be rented out or lent?

Rental, as for all other copyright works, is an exclusive right of the copyright owner and this includes the renting out of works in electronic form and computer programs. Lending is permitted but public libraries can lend e-books only if they are covered by PLR or an agreement with the publisher. From a legal point of view, computer programs and works in electronic form can be lent. For example, it should be possible to lend a CD-ROM within the limits for lending specified in Sections 4.65 and following.

11.43   Supposing a library has a work in electronic form and another library wants to consult it. Can the second library be given access for a limited time?

Probably not. The contract giving access will define who can use a particular electronic work.

Publication right

11.44   Are electronic materials generally subject to publication right?

Theoretically, yes, but where do you find such materials out of copyright?!

Communication to the public right

11.45   Is this right applicable to electronic materials?

Yes. In a nutshell it allows the copyright owner to control putting the work onto a website, and therefore plugs the hole in the law which excludes transmission of a website from the definition of a broadcast.

11.46   What is the actual definition of this right?

The definition of 'communication to the public right' is:

- broadcasting the work
- making the work available by electronic transmission so that members of the public may access it from a place and at a time individually chosen by them.

Performance

11.47   Are the rights of performance relevant to electronic materials?

Yes, in two respects. First, the content of an electronic document may be multimedia in nature with songs, speeches or dancing. These all have rights of performance in them. Second, performers now enjoy a separate right to prevent their performances being made available on the internet without their permission. This is called making available right.

11.48   What exactly is making available right?

It is defined as the right 'to prevent anyone making available to the public a recording of a performance by electronic transmission so that members of the public may access the recording from a place and at a time chosen by them'.

Duration

11.49   How long does copyright in an electronic work last?

So far as the content is concerned, the same rules apply as if the work were not electronic.

11.50 **But if a new edition of a work causes a new term of copyright, what constitutes a new edition of an electronically stored work?**

That is difficult to decide. Obviously if a whole new piece is added then the work is a new edition but if, as in the case of a database, material is added frequently, and in small pieces, it is difficult to say whether every addition creates a new edition or whether a lot of new data has to be added before this can be claimed. A further problem is that no actual printed version is made every time a change is made so some editions may come and go and never be known about. Special rules apply to databases.

Fair dealing

11.51 **Is there fair dealing in electronic works?**

This is not an easy question to answer. Technically there is fair dealing in the content of any electronic work where that content qualifies for fair dealing. However, as electronic works can be accessed usually only by the use of passwords and a contract with the supplier, this contract cannot override the privileges granted by Parliament for fair dealing and other exceptions. Any clause that purports to do this is considered null and void. A further consideration is to take into account what is 'fair' in electronic terms. Fair dealing is not limited to copying, but this is the most usual form that it takes. But the idea of 'fair' (see Section 4.134 and following) may be difficult to justify in an electronic world, when it is so easy to *exactly* reproduce a work, store and retransmit it and even change it.

Educational use

11.52 **Can electronic materials be used for educational purposes?**

If they were acquired in electronic form, then they can be used for illustrating a lesson either by the teacher or the student within the limits of what is considered fair. In the case of virtual learning environment (VLE) work, when a group of students signs up for work carried out in a VLE environment they should understand that any work they put up on the server can be used, modified or commented on by any other member of the virtual or managed learning environment group. Retention of the work beyond the lifespan of the group would be an infringement. It would also be an infringement to put the work up on the internet or intranet site of the whole university or college, as this would be communicating the work to the public by electronic means.

11.53 **What about putting theses or dissertations on to the internet?**

While this might be allowed for the text prepared by the student, the copyright in any copyright material included in the thesis as allowed for educational purposes (see Section 4.177) would be infringed. This should not be done except with the permission of the original copyright owner, as this would be communicating the work to the public by electronic means.

Other purposes

11.54 **For what other purposes does fair dealing apply?**

The law permits use of electronic materials for criticism, quotation or review and reporting current events in just the same way as other materials. Remember that reporting for current events excludes the use of photographs.

11.55 **Are there other limitations?**

The rules for use of copyright materials for public administration and disabled people are the same.

Protection mechanisms

11.56 **But some electronic documents can be accessed only by using a password or giving your credit card number. Is this legal?**

Yes, the law specifically protects the use of effective technological measures to protect electronic materials.

11.57 **What does 'effective technological measure' actually mean?**

If use of the work is controlled by the copyright owner through an access control or protection process such as encryption, scrambling or other transformation of the work, or a copy control mechanism that achieves the intended protection, then the protection mechanism is considered an effective one.

11.58 **What difference does this make?**

A lot, because it is an offence (and this can be criminal) to circumvent such effective protection mechanisms and the copyright owner has the same redress as if the copyright of the work itself were infringed.

11.59   **But could this stop someone from exercising the privileges they have under fair dealing or use by a disabled person?**

Any clause in a contract governing access to material which prevents acts allowed by this legislation is considered void.

11.60   **Are there other protection mechanisms?**

Yes, the other mechanism is referred to as Electronic Rights Management System (ERMS).

11.61   **What is an ERMS?**

An ERMS is defined in law as 'any information provided by the copyright owner which identifies the work, the author or any other right holder, or information about the terms and conditions of use of the work, and any numbers or codes that represent such information'.

11.62   **Are these data protected by law?**

Yes, it is an offence to remove the data (which is usually encoded using metadata tags) or transmit the document to a third party without the data.

11.63   **But could this stop someone enjoying the exceptions set out in the other chapters such as fair dealing or use by disabled people?**

Yes.

11.64   **What can be done in these circumstances?**

Where this circumstance arises the IPO provides a complaint form on their website: https://assets.publishing.service.gov.uk/government/uploads/system/uploads/attachment_data/file/457660/Notice-of_TPM-compaints.pdf (consulted November 2018).

Websites

11.65   **Do websites present any particular problems?**

Websites present all kinds of copyright problems The paragraphs below give some indication of the problems libraries may face when considering using website technology to develop their services. You need to consider who owns the website and whether the website constitutes a database as defined in law. Other issues include the status of a website (whether a broadcast or a cable programme service) and liability of website providers.

11.66 Is it an infringement to put works on the internet or world wide web?

Yes. This infringes the right of communication of the work to the public by electronic means.

11.67 But supposing a document is put on the web but nobody ever downloads it. Is this still an infringement?

Yes, because the document has been made available to the public by electronic means. The fact that nobody accesses the work is another matter. It is an infringement of communication to the public right, even if this is done without charge, unless the person issuing the copies has the right to do so. The fact that nobody ever reads these copies is irrelevant!

11.68 Does the fact that it is so easy to build links to other websites pose any problems?

Possibly. It depends on whether you build your link to the home page of the other website, build deep links (direct into the text of the other website), use framed links (which bring up a framed image, which does not make clear whose property it actually is) or embedded links (where an actual image from another website is embedded in your own to make the link direct). If you build a direct ('deep') link you should always give the user the option of finding the home page as well. Embedded links are to be avoided, as the use of the logo from another organisation could infringe their trademark rights as well as implying approval of the website about which they may know nothing.

11.69 Why go to so much trouble?

There are several reasons:

- Website owners may not wish their website to be associated with yours. You may be promoting views with which they strongly disagree.
- You may bypass important information about ownership, conditions of use and even advertising, all of which the user would have found on the home page.
- If the user does not perceive that the information is owned by and made

available through a different website provider from the one where she or he began the search, that user may think the material is owned or supplied by the original website to which they logged on. This can cause the library to be accused of 'passing-off' – making services available which users think come from the library when, in fact, they belong to someone else.

11.70 What about subscription websites?

It is an infringement of copyright to make a link from one website to another when the latter is protected by password or subscription, as this by-passes the need to register or log in and therefore deprives the copyright owner of income and control over who accesses the material.

11.71 Some websites have an icon to click for copyright information. Is this legal or necessary?

It is very necessary to ensure that users know exactly who owns what and what they can do with material located. The icon prevents the user claiming ignorance of either ownership or conditions. Where websites start with a statement such as 'By clicking on this icon you agree that you have read the conditions of use and copyright statement' then the user is bound by those conditions and cannot plead ignorance.

11.72 Is all material on the web copyright?

Probably. To be safe, behave with material on the web as if it were in paper form. If you would not copy or distribute it in paper form, then do not do so in electronic form, unless the owner specifically states this can be done, which many website owners do.

11.73 What about older text such as medieval manuscripts, which have been put on the web by major libraries or archives?

The original text may be out of copyright but the electronic version almost certainly attracts its own copyright, as it will have been created as a result of extensive research, editing and correction. Electronic images are rarely in a sufficiently good state to be mounted without careful attention, so a new copyright work has been created (but see Section 2.3). In addition, most such websites probably qualify for protection as databases, as they should meet the definition of a database (see Section 9.1). They are pretty poor websites if they do not, so extraction and reuse of substantial parts of it would be excluded. However, if there is no copyright in the original material then there is no infringement of the communication to the public right.

11.74 Do most copyright rules apply to websites or are there special issues to consider?

The answers to many copyright questions that arise in the electronic world are exactly the same as those to the questions that arise in the more traditional paper-based world. However, some issues are peculiar to electronic materials and some of the answers which are clear in the paper world are not so obvious when we deal with electronic materials. The legislation on databases makes many of the answers different if the work is considered a database.

Open access

11.75 What is open access?

Open access is defined by the Jisc of the universities as what 'occurs when full-text journal articles, plus other research information . . . are made freely available on-line'.

11.76 Does this mean the material made available can be used in any way?

No. It simply means that access is free but, unless otherwise stated, the material is protected just like any other copyright material, and the usual rules apply.

Social media websites

11.77 There are lots of websites now where individuals can post their own writings, photos, videos or recordings of songs. Are these protected by copyright?

Yes. Anything that you create as an individual and put up on any of these sites, chatrooms or blogs is technically your property.

11.78 Can I stop other people downloading and re-using it?

By putting material into these types of website you must be aware that other people will download this material and therefore you have given an implied licence for them to do this.

11.79   Can they use my material to make their own postings or other works?

No. That would be a clear infringement, especially if they actually published your photos, words or films.

11.80   What is the position if the video I post on one of these websites contains copyright work such as songs, music playing in the background or even a photo of a painting from other people?

This is something you must try to avoid because it infringes the copyright in the music, song or painting, and may infringe the performing rights of the musicians and the copyright in the recording. Similarly, staff in any library or information service must be extremely careful if they download and circulate any material from these kinds of websites, as it may contain infringing material, which could cause them to be accused of illegally publishing the material and circulating it.

Below are listed some of the more common websites (in summer 2019), but others are appearing all the time and it is important to check what each one says about copyright if you intend to make material available through them or use them as a source of information.

11.81   YouTube

The YouTube website has copyright tips to help you avoid infringing copyright; if material is found to be infringing, there is a proper procedure to notify YouTube that the material is infringing and should be taken down. Video clips are particularly vulnerable to including copyright material such as music and recordings, so take particular care when posting something and also using anything you find on YouTube.

11.82   Is material on Wikipedia protected by copyright?

The Wikipedia website (as at autumn 2018) says:

> Wikipedia's textual content is copyrighted, but you may reuse it under the terms of our licensing requirements, summarised below.
>
> Most text in Wikipedia, excluding quotations, has been released under the Creative Commons Attribution-ShareAlike 3.0 Unported Licence (CC-BY-SA) and the GNU Free Documentation License (GFDL) (unversioned, with no invariant sections, front-cover texts, or back-cover texts) and can therefore be reused only if you release any derived work

under the Creative Commons Attribution/Share-Alike License or the GFDL. This requires that, among other things, you attribute the authors and allow others to freely copy your work. (See Wikipedia: Text of Creative Commons Attribution-ShareAlike 3.0 Unported License and Wikipedia: Text of the GNU Free Documentation License for full details.) See https://en.wikipedia.org/wiki/Wikipedia:Copyrights for more specific details (consulted 5.9.2018)

Some material on Wikipedia, for example images, may have their own licensing conditions, which must be observed.

11.83   Do authors have to sign up to these conditions?

No, but by agreeing to contribute they give an implied licence to use their work under the GNU Free Documentation Licence. You cannot contribute to Wikipedia without agreeing to this.

11.84   Flickr

Flickr is a photo-sharing website, which allows participants to share their photos with other members. Copyright remains with the photographer, but if any participant considers their work has been unfairly copied and reused, or other IPRs have been infringed, Flickr has an online complaint form through which action can be taken to have the member who has infringed barred or their material blocked. Flickr has an excellent 'dos' and 'don'ts' page called Community Guidelines, which gives useful guidance. See www.flickr.com/help/guidelines (consulted 5 September 2018).

11.85   Facebook

Facebook's mission is to give people the power to share and make the world more open and connected and to keep up with friends, upload an unlimited number of photos, share links and videos, and learn more about the people they meet. The Facebook website states that Facebook respects the intellectual property rights of others and is committed to helping third parties protect their rights. Their Statement of Rights and Responsibilities prohibits users from posting content that violates another party's IPR. When Facebook receives a valid notice of intellectual property infringement, they promptly remove or disable access to the allegedly infringing content. They will also terminate the accounts of repeat infringers in appropriate circumstances. Rights holders will find information regarding how to report copyright and other intellectual property infringements by users posting content on their website, and answers to some frequently asked questions regarding their policies, at www.facebook.com/help/intellectual_property (consulted 5 September 2018).

11.86 Pinterest

Like other social media websites, Pinterest has a section on its website about copyright. There are some differences, which anyone pinning an image should notice. While there is no assertion by Pinterest of copyright ownership over content that a user posts to Pinterest, by using the service a user grants Pinterest and its users a non-exclusive, royalty-free, transferable, sub-licensable, worldwide licence to use, store, display, reproduce, re-pin, modify, create derivative works, perform and distribute the user's content on Pinterest for the purposes of operating, developing, providing and using the Pinterest products. For more details see https://policy.pinterest.com/en-gb/terms-of-service (consulted 5 September 2018).

11.87 Twitter

Twitter has a statement about copyright on its website that it will take action if infringement can be shown, but there are strong arguments that many tweets cannot be copyright because they are not original but repeats of what has been said elsewhere, whether on Twitter or not. Also the limited length of the tweet makes it harder to show creativity (but certainly not impossible!) and that is a crucial element in copyright. Twitter has an extensive copyright policy and general guidance for users although much of it is framed in terms of US copyright law. See https://help.twitter.com/en/rules-and-policies#general-policies (consulted 5 September 2018).

11.88 Instagram

Instagram is a photo-sharing website making it easier to share photographs across different platforms and devices. It has extensive copyright guidance at https://help.instagram.com/126382350847838 (consulted 5 September 2018).

Section 12
Other matters

International treaties

12.1 What importance does international copyright have?

Technically there is no such thing as 'international copyright'. Each country has its own copyright laws but nearly all countries belong to some or all of the three international conventions. Under these treaties and conventions each country protects the works produced in other countries as if they had been produced within its own borders, although usually works are not protected in a country for longer than they would be in the country of origin. So if a work is produced in a country where protection lasts for 50 years but is imported into a country where protection lasts for 70 years, then the work would still be protected for only 50 years in that country.

12.2 Which are these three major conventions?

The Berne Copyright Convention, the Universal Copyright Convention (UCC) and the Trade Related Intellectual Property element of the World Trade Agreement. A fourth, the World Intellectual Property Organization (WIPO) Copyright Treaty, was agreed in 1996. There are also international treaties covering sound recordings (phonographs), film and video and copying material for visually impaired people and others with print disabilities.

12.3 Are there any countries which do not belong to any of these conventions?

Yes, but the number is decreasing all the time. Those where representatives have not signed one or more treaties cannot benefit from the liberalisation of trade planned under the World Trade Agreement, so there is an incentive to reform or improve national copyright laws in most countries.

12.4   If a country does not belong to one of these treaties does this mean that its publications can be copied?

Perhaps. Although not all countries belong to one of the international treaties, one or two have signed bilateral agreements with the UK for mutual protection. It is best to check the latest SI (see Section 1).

12.5   What is the importance of the copyright symbol (ã)?

The idea of the ã symbol is to indicate the work was protected by copyright in the country of origin and has been registered for copyright protection. This is important under the UCC as publications without the symbol are not regarded as protected. The symbol is chiefly important on publications from those countries that belong to the UCC but not to Berne. It also protects publications in those same UCC countries, so it is important for publishers to include it on their works even if it is not required in the country of origin, as it should protect them when exported to UCC countries. Lack of the symbol in most countries has no significance. Note that there are now very few countries that belong to the UCC but not to Berne and/or the World Trade Organization.

Legal deposit

12.6   What is the connection between legal deposit and copyright law?

None, nor has there been for many years. Copyright deposit is there to enable the designated libraries to build up collections of the publicly available material produced in the UK. The law was radically revised in 2003 under the Legal Deposit Act 2003, which includes enabling legislation to protect and manage copyright for electronic materials deposited with the designated libraries. These are the British Library, the National Library of Scotland, the National Library of Wales, the Bodleian Library in Oxford, Cambridge University Library and the Library of Trinity College, Dublin.

12.7   Why do some people still call it 'copyright deposit'?

Because it used to be a prerequisite for being able to claim copyright. The law on legal deposit was enshrined in the Copyright Act of 1911, hence this misnomer has continued for many years. But international conventions require that no formality of any kind is necessary before claiming copyright. The term 'copyright deposit' is now obsolete and 'legal deposit' should be used instead.

12.8   Can disabled people access legal deposit material in formats they need?

Yes, provided certain limitations are observed, which the appropriate deposit library provides if asked. Specifically, providing different formats is not allowed for databases.

12.9   Is there a connection between PLR and copyright?

Yes. This was not true until the introduction of the lending or rental legislation, but PLR and copyright are now firmly linked.

12.10   What is the connection between ISBNs, ISSNs and copyright?

Absolutely none. ISBNs (International Standard Book Numbers), ISSNs (International Standard Serial Numbers) and similar numbering systems are essentially tools of the bookselling and publishing industry, which have been hijacked by librarians as useful systems for cataloguing, identifying and locating. Their presence or absence from a document has no bearing on its copyright status.

Droit de suite or resale right

12.11   There has been a lot of talk about a right called 'droit de suite'. What is it?

Droit de suite is a right given to the creator of an original work of art (painting, sculpture, etc.) so that each time the work is sold the creator gets a percentage of the increased price, if there is one. Thus a painter who starts off as unknown and sells paintings for a few pounds can benefit from any subsequent fame achieved.

12.12   Does this have anything to do with libraries or archives?

Only if they have, or plan to acquire, collections of original works of art.

12.13   Has this right been introduced into the UK?

Yes. It was implemented in 2006 but did not come into force until 2010. It applies to most artistic works that are resold after 2010, but excludes any private sales.

Other legislation

12.14 Human rights laws in the UK guarantee individuals the right of free speech. They also protect family life and personal privacy. Can copyright be seen as infringing human rights?

No, because the assertion of the right of free speech cannot be used to take away private property from someone else. As copyright is a property law, you can express yourself in any legal way you wish but not use someone else's property to do it. However, see Section 5.15 for important comments on photographs and privacy.

12.15 How does copyright interact with data protection?

Although most data covered by the Data Protection Act is liable to database right, the rights conferred by the Data Protection Act do not change the rights of owners of database right at all.

12.16 What about FOI laws?

Again, rights of access to information do not change the rights of owners of the copyright in that information. FOI does not mean that information is delivered free of charge. See Section 4.309 for more detailed information.

Useful addresses and contacts

Authors' Licensing and Collecting Society
      1st Floor
      Barnard's Inn
      86 Fetter Lane
      London
      EC4A 1EN
      Tel: 020 7264 5700
      E-mail: alcs@alcs.co.uk
      Website: www.alcs.co.uk

British Copyright Council
      2 Pancras Square
      London
      N1C 4AG
      Tel: 020 3290 1444
      E-mail: info@britishcopyright.org
      Website: www.britishcopyright.org.uk

Christian Copyright Licensing International (CCLI)
      Chantry House
      22 Upperton Road
      Eastbourne
      East Sussex BN21 1BF
      Tel: 01323 436100 (customers)
      Tel: 01323 436104 (copyright owners)
      Website: www.ccli.com.

CILIP: the Library and Information Association

> 7 Ridgmount Street
> London WC1E 7AE
> Tel: 020 7255 0500
> E-mail: info@cilip.org.uk
> Website: www.cilip.org.uk

Copyright Licensing Agency

> Barnard's Inn,
> 86 Fetter Lane,
> London, EC4A 1EN
> Tel: 020 7400 3100
> E-mail: cla@cla.co.uk
> Website: www.cla.co.uk

Design and Artists Copyright Society

> 33 Old Bethnal Green Road
> London E2 6AA
> Tel: 020 7336 8811
> Fax: 020 7336 8822
> E-mail: info@dacs.org.uk
> Website: www.dacs.org.uk

Educational Recording Agency

> Barnard's Inn,
> 86 Fetter Lane,
> London, EC4A 1EN
> Tel: 020 7837 6222
> E-mail: era@era.org.uk

HMSO

> See The National Archives

Motion Picture Licensing Corporation

MPLC House
4 Saffrons Road
Eastbourne
East Sussex BN21 1DQ
Tel: 01323 649647
E-mail: ukinfo@mplc.com
Website: themplc.co.uk

Music Publishers Association

2 Pancras Square
London
N1C 4AG
Tel: 020 3741 3800
E-mail: info@mpaonline.org.uk
Website: www.mpaonline.org.uk

The National Archives and HMSO

Kew
Richmond
Surrey TW9 4DU
Tel: 020 8876 3444
Website: www.nationalarchives.gov.uk

Newspaper Licensing Agency

Mount Pleasant House
Lonsdale Gardens
Tunbridge Wells
Kent TN1 1HJ
Tel: 01892 525 273
Fax: 01892 525 275
E-mail: copy@nla.co.uk
Website: www.nlamediaaccess.com

Ordnance Survey

Explorer House
Adanac Drive
Southampton SO16 0AS
Tel: 03456 050505
Website: www.ordnancesurvey.co.uk

Ordnance Survey Northern Ireland

[now part of Land and Property Services of Northern Ireland]
Lanyon Plaza
7 Lanyon Place
Town Parks
Belfast BT1 3LP
Tel: 0300 200 7804 (within Northern Ireland)
Website: www.dfpni.gov.uk

Phonographic Performance Ltd

1 Upper James Street
London W1F 9DE
Tel: 020 7534 1000
E-mail: info@ppluk.com
Website: www.ppluk.com

PRS for Music

2 Pancras Square
London
N1C 4AG
Tel: 020 7580 5544
Website: www.prsformusic.com

Public Lending Right Office

Richard House
Sorbonne Close
Stockton-on-Tees TS17 6DA
Tel: 01642 604699
Website: www.plr.uk.com

Public Video Screening Licence [Filmbank]

Warner House
90 Theobald's Road
London WC1X 8WB
Tel: 020 7984 5950
E-mail: info@filmbank.co.uk
Website: www.filmbank.co.uk

Useful sources of information

Some useful books, journals and websites are listed below. A consolidated version of the CDPA can be found at www.legislation.gov.uk/ukpga/1988/48/contents.

Several legal publishers produce consolidated acts, usually published with other intellectual property law.

When looking for books on copyright, note the publication date of the latest edition as this affects how up to date the information is.

In the list below titles marked * after the ISBN are very useful for general principles and many aspects of copyright law, but do not contain details of the changes made in 2014.

Books

Caddick, Nicholas, Davies, Gillian and Harbottle, Gwilym (2019) *Copinger and Skone James on Copyright*, 17th edn, two volumes and supplement, London, Sweet & Maxwell, ISBN 9780414064300.

Cornish, Graham P. (2013) *Keeping it Legal: copyright guidance for school library staff*, Swindon, School Library Association, ISBN 9781903446751*.

Flint, Michael F., Thorne, Clive, and Cornthwaite Jonathan (2017) *A User's Guide to Copyright*, 7th edn, London, Bloomsbury Publishing, ISBN 9781847666857*.

Groves, Peter (2011) *Dictionary of Intellectual Property Law*, Cheltenham, Edward Elgar Publishing, ISBN 9781849807777*.

Laddie, Hugh, et al. (2000) *The Modern Law of Copyright and Designs*, 3rd edn (3 vols), London, Butterworth, ISBN 0406903832*. Although this appears rather dated it is invaluable for interpreting case law.

Oppenheim, Charles (2012) *The No-Nonsense Guide to Legal Issues in Web 2.0 and Cloud Computing*, London, Facet Publishing, ISBN 9781856048040*.

Padfield, Tim (2015) *Copyright for Archivists and Records Managers*, 5th edn, London, Facet Publishing, ISBN 9781856049290.

Pedley, Paul (2008) *Copyright Compliance: practical steps to stay within the law*, London, Facet Publishing, ISBN 9781856046404*.

Pedley, Paul (2012) *Essential Law for Information Professionals*, 3rd edn, London, Facet Publishing, ISBN 9781856047692. Covers a wide range of legal issues, of which copyright is just one.

Pedley, Paul (2012) *The E-copyright Handbook*, London, Facet Publishing, ISBN 9781856048279*.

Pedley, Paul (2015) *Practical Copyright for Library and Information Professionals*, London, Facet Publishing, ISBN 9781783300617.

Phillips, Jeremy (2017) *Butterworth Intellectual Property Law Handbook*, 13th edn, London, Butterworth, ISBN 9781474307031.

Secker, Jane, with Chris Morrison (2016) *Copyright and E-learning*, 2nd edn, London, Facet Publishing, ISBN 9781783300600.

Stokes, Simon (2012) *Art and Copyright*, 2nd edn, Oxford, Hart Publishing, ISBN paperback 9781849461627; Adobe PDF e-book 9781847318954; e-Pub 9781847318961*.

Stokes, Simon (2014) *Digital Copyright: law and practice*, Oxford, Hart Publishing, ISBN hardback 9781849464024, e-Pub 9781782252535.

Periodicals

Copyright Bulletin. Published online by Unesco, Paris. Archival issues accessible free online. http://unesdoc.unesco.org/ulis/copyright/search.htm.

European Intellectual Property Review. Published monthly by Sweet & Maxwell.

Intellectual Property Magazine. Available online at www.intellectualpropertymagazine.com

Websites

www.copyrightcircle.co.uk
https://archive.cilip.org.uk/research/topics/copyright/laca-libraries-archives-copyright-alliance.
The website for the Library and Archive Copyright Alliance, which brings together most of the major players in the information provision industry to discuss copyright.

www.ipo.gov.uk
A website maintained by the Intellectual Property Office to give information

on a wide range of intellectual property issues. Copyright is well covered and there is a frequently asked questions page as well as guidance notes.

www.wipo.int

To keep up with international developments in the World Intellectual Property Organization.

www.eblida.org

Useful for European developments, especially relating to libraries.

www.bbc.co.uk/news.

Surprisingly useful for latest news on copyright, especially in the media.

www.nationalarchives.gov.uk/information-management/re-using-public-sector-information/copyright/crown-copyright

Latest information on use of Crown copyright material.

www.cla.co.uk

The website for the CLA.

www.nla.co.uk

The website for the NLA.

www.alcs.co.uk

The Authors' Licensing and Collection Society website has links to all other licensing agencies in the UK.

Crackingideas.com

A website aimed at teachers and pupils in schools.

CopyrightUser.org.uk

This is an resource aimed at making UK Copyright Law accessible to creators, media professionals, entrepreneurs, students, and the public. Numerous clearly-described case studies.

https:\\copyrightliteracy.org.uk

'Decoding copyright and bringing you enlightenment'.

Appendix: suggested declaration forms

Declaration: copy of article or part of published work

To the [name of supplying organisation]_____

Name of person requesting the copy_____

1.   Please supply me with a copy of:
       *the article in the periodical, the particulars of which are [   ]
       *the part of the published work, the particulars of which are [   ] required by me
       for the purposes of non-commercial research or private study.

2.   I declare that:

(a)   I have not previously been supplied with a copy of the same material by you or any
       library;

(b)   I require the copy for research for a non-commercial purpose or private study, will
       use it only for those purposes and will not supply the copy to any other person; and

(c)   to the best of my knowledge no other person with whom I work or study has made
       or intends to make, at or about the same time as this request, a request for
       substantially the same material for substantially the same purpose.

Declaration: copy of the whole or part of unpublished work

To the [name of supplying organisation]_____

Name of person requesting the copy_____

1.　　Please supply me with a copy of all or part of:

　　　the unpublished work, the particulars of which are [　　] required by me for the

　　　purposes of non-commercial research or private study.

2.　　I declare that:

(a)　　I have not previously been supplied with a copy of the same material by you or any

　　　library or archive.

(b)　　I require the copy for research for a non-commercial purpose or private study, will

　　　use it only for those purposes and will not supply the copy to any other person.

Index